MICHAE...
HI...

MICHAEL COLLINS HIMSELF

CHRISSY OSBORNE

MERCIER PRESS

MERCIER PRESS
Douglas Village, Cork
www.mercierpress.ie

Trade enquiries to COLUMBA MERCIER DISTRIBUTION,
55a Spruce Avenue, Stillorgan Industrial Park, Blackrock, Dublin

© Chrissy Osborne, 2003

ISBN: 978 1 85635 407 3

10 9 8 7

ACKNOWLEDGMENTS
The author and publisher would like to thank the following for permission to use their
photographs: National Museum of Ireland, National Library of Ireland, Michael Griffin:
Michael Collins Association, London, Kevin Coleman, Cathal Brugha Barracks, Brendan Leigh
Doyle, the Kiernan family, the Collins family, Fionnuala Donovan, Peg O'Driscoll, Lisbeth Kelly,
Melissa Llewelyn Davis and Eileen Cooke (Howth).
Every effort has been made to establish the sources of all the photographs used and acknow-
ledgement given – should a source have not been acknowledged, we take this opportunity of
apologising for such an oversight and will make the necessary correction at the first
opportunity.

Printed in Ireland by Colour Books Ltd.

CONTENTS

DEDICATED TO

MY FATHER WHO FIRST KINDLED MY LOVE FOR IRELAND AND ITS HISTORY

FOREWORD

This affectionate collection of Michael Collins memorabilia by Chrissy Osborne creates a gentle picture of some of the man's more ordinary and more endearing traits. Anecdotes about his family background, his taste in clothes, culture and how he amused himself, predominate over accounts of guerrilla warfare or high politics.

As the text is illustrated, the work adds up to a nice present for anyone already interested in the great Irish leader or a useful introduction to Collins' life for someone who has heard the name but knows little of the man. And more should be known about Collins, not merely as a mythic figure from the past. He has a very direct and instructional relevance to the present also. To think of him limed merely in a family glow, as it were, would be akin to basing one's impressions of his beloved West Cork coastline on a summer holiday spent sailing from places like Clonakilty, Union Hall, Baltimore or even Schull, along by the Fastnet, without even knowing what the area looked like in a winter storm. Or knowing only that Collins' great adversary, Winston Churchill, smoked cigars, wore boiler suits, kept black swans and painted pictures.

For example, as Chrissy Osborne points out, an important element in Collins' character formation was the fact that his father, a remarkably learned man and respected figure, was seventy-five when Collins was born, the youngest of a large family, as intelligent as it was adoring. Collins senior had lived through the famine, a traumatic event, which evidently influenced him, as it did hundreds of thousands of others then and subsequently, to delay marrying and bringing children into such a cruel and unpredictable world. Many of the elder Collins' contemporaries never got over that fear and did not marry at all. For several decades after Michael Collins' death, the elderly Irish bachelor, living alone, was a common sight in the Irish countryside.

Stories of the famine, of the fenians and of the land war that raged through Cork with particular virulence, not all that long before Collins' birth, were staples of the conversations which the young Michael Collins heard at home, school and pre-television, at that great source of information, the forge.

All these things helped to shape his political outlook and led, through the GPO, to the formation of his assassination squad, 'the twelve apostles', guerrilla warfare, the Treaty, on which contemporary Ireland is founded, and his Janus faced policy towards Northern Ireland: he armed the IRA there while seeking to crush the organisation in the south and used every means in his power to de-stabilise the new statelet.

The complexities, injustices, intrigues and the detritus of empire which led to the formulation of this duplicitous policy are still with us. The Good Friday Agreement, the contemporary variant of Collins' Treaty, which was supposed to help resolve these complexities, is tottering. Elections have been postponed, as Britain once again ignores majority opinion on the island of Ireland and tilts towards supporting, not even Unionism, but a mere fragment of it, that led by David Trimble. Many of the attitudes and the forces which go to create today's six county impasse were present in Collins' day and drove him to act as he did.

The moral of the story, even a gently told and domestic one, like that recounted in the following pages, is an old one – those who do not learn from history, relive it.

TIM PAT COOGAN

The young Michael, aged about eleven, with his mother, grandmother and sister Mary outside the 'new' house at Woodfield, circa 1901

INTRODUCTION

Having been born and lived most of my life in England, people have often asked me, as an Englishwoman, why I have become so fascinated by Michael Collins. However, like 50% of the population in that country, my roots are in Ireland. My family, on my father's side, were originally from Kilgarrif, a townland just outside of Clonakilty in West Cork, and just a couple of miles from Woodfield, where Michael Collins was born in 1890. One of the many interesting links between Michael and myself, I discovered during my research into this book, was that a great-uncle of his, and a great, great, great-uncle of mine, had been next door neighbours, both living in Kilgarrif during the mid nineteenth century.

From around the early 1950s, I was to spend many annual family holidays in Ireland, usually in the south, although we did have one, touring around County Down and the Mourne Mountains, just before the new 'troubles' erupted in the early 1960s.

Boarding the train, which, in the 1950s was hauled by a giant steam locomotive, at Euston Station, London, we would arrive some hours later at Holyhead in North Wales. At that time, the train pulled up next to the dock, and its passengers, including myself and family, would then alight, and walk over to the waiting steamer, either the *RMS Hibernia* or its sister ship *Cambria*. The steamer, or 'mail' boat, which was its main function, was also capable of carrying up to 2,000-foot passengers – car ferries were still a thing of the future. The voyage across the Irish Sea to Dun Laoghaire took about four hours on a good run, and as we neared the coast of Ireland most of the passengers came up on deck, to catch a first glimpse of their beloved homeland.

Occasionally, my parents decided to spend a couple of days in Dublin, before heading off by train to the west of Ireland, where we usually spent our holidays.

My earliest memories of Dublin were of numerous horse-drawn vehicles, and very few cars. In fact, I vividly remember having just caught the train up from Dun Laoghaire to Westland Row station, now Pearse Street, coming out of the terminus with my parents, and climbing into a waiting horse-drawn hackney cab. I can still recall the dark, leathery smell of its interior, and the ensuing bumpy journey, as horse and vehicle clattered across the city's cobbled streets, to the hotel we were staying at in Mountjoy Street. However, forty-five years ago, I never knew that we were just a stone's throw from where Michael Collins had lived at No. 44. The area, in Dublin's north inner city, even by the mid 1950s, would have changed very little from the time when Michael had resided there between 1917 and 1919.

I also remember, although I was only about seven at the time, the run-down tenements and slums that had once been the smart town houses of the wealthy of Dublin, back in the late Georgian and early Victorian era. Although living conditions were beginning to improve by the 1950s, there was still a great deal of poverty in

Dublin's inner city. It was in Dublin that, for the first time, I had ever seen children playing in the streets bare-footed and badly clad. Despite being only a young child myself, it was a memory that was to remain with me for the rest of my life.

From the mid 1950s to the mid 1960s, I was fortunate to spend many an idyllic holiday, with friends of my parents, on a remote farm in the foothills of Ireland's highest mountain Carrauntouhil, which is part of the Macgillycuddy Reeks in Co. Kerry. The farm, run by three elderly sisters, had been in the family for generations. Most of their relations had either emigrated or died, and the day-to-day running of the farm had changed very little in the last hundred years. There was no electricity or running water, and all the cooking was done over an open fire in the main living-room / kitchen. The turf, which was our only fuel and source of heating, was cut from the bogs on the mountain slopes behind us. The farm was completely self-sufficient. The milk from the cows was churned into butter. The fleece from the sheep was carded and spun, to make wool for clothing. Hens provided us with fresh eggs and the pig, having been killed by the local travelling butcher, would be cured, to provide our weekly supply of rashers and boiled bacon. The few luxuries, such as soap or fruit, would arrive about once a fortnight, via the travelling shop, weather permitting. Each Sunday morning we would set off down Black Valley, by pony and trap, along the rough track that led to the nearest village, about five miles away. Here, we would attend mass, which in those days was in Latin, at the village church. Occasionally, during the evening, some of the local neighbours would arrive at the farm and we would have an impromptu 'ceilidhe'. Fiddles and tin whistles would come out, and we would sing and dance, often into the early hours of the morning. Many of the old songs and tunes that we sang had been handed down from past generations, some having reference to the terrible days of the Great Famine. Black Valley and the immediate area around it saw some of the worst scenes of evictions, starvation and death in the county of Kerry.

It is only now, some forty years later, that I realised how privileged I was to have experienced such a way of life, even though it was only for a few weeks each year. This simple, old-fashioned life-style I am sure has now disappeared forever, even in the remotest parts of Ireland. In many ways, it would have been very similar to the world Michael Collins' had known and grown up in, as a young boy in West Cork in the 1890s.

It was also during those childhood, and later teenage, holidays in Ireland, that I was to develop a great love for all things Irish, its music, culture and history, although then, I only had a passing interest in Ireland's more recent past. My father, however, had a keen interest in its history and especially the 1916–22 period. He often spoke about De Valera and Michael Collins, although at the time, their names meant little to me. My father also had a fair knowledge of the Irish language, along with being a skilful 'step' dancer – all abilities inherited from his Irish roots.

By the late 1960s however, my family and life saw many changes. Our annual holidays to Ireland had ended. I had left home and gone to live in Canada and my parents, whose health had begun to deteriorate, were unable to undertake the long and arduous journey over to Ireland ever again.

It was after an absence of almost thirty years, that I eventually returned to a very different Ireland in 1996. It had joined the European Union and under its influence had become, at last, a prosperous and dynamic country – the Celtic Tiger had arrived! It was also during that holiday, an event happened that was to change my life.

In the spring of 1996, myself along with my husband and two friends decided to take a holiday in the west of Ireland, touring around the still remote region of Connemara. We drove through the wild and rugged countryside, on what was a beautiful, sunny May day, until we reached Clifden, a small market town nestling in the foothills of the mountains. Here, we decided to stop for lunch and have a look around the place.

Leaving my husband and friends at the local general outfitters, sifting through the Aran sweaters and Donegal tweed jackets and caps, I strolled on down the main street, stopping in front of the town's only bookshop. Prominently displayed in the shop window, was Tim Pat Coogan's recent biography of Michael Collins. On the front cover of the book, was a head and shoulders photograph of Michael, taken, I was to discover later, when he became chairman of the new Provisional Government in January 1922. It immediately struck me – what an interesting, and handsome, character he looked. I went into the shop and, flicking through the pages of the book, quickly realised just what an intriguing, indeed amazing person this Michael Collins actually was.

Back in England, after the holiday, I bought Tim Pat's book, as it had been republished to coincide with Neil Jordan's film *Michael Collins*, due to be released later that same year. I read the book within a couple of weeks and immediately

Where it all began in 1996!

became totally fascinated with this charismatic Irishman and all he had done for his country in the early part of the twentieth century.

It was from that point on my whole life began to change. I returned to Ireland several times over the next four years, each time seeking to learn more about this Michael Collins and discovering the various places associated with him. Beautiful West Cork was where he was born and reared, the numerous safe-houses and offices scattered around Dublin, used by him between 1917 and 1921, as well as the more remote associations with him, such as Sligo Jail where he was imprisoned for three weeks, and the Greville Arms in Granard, Co. Longford, home of Kitty Kiernan, the woman he finally fell madly in love with, and had hoped to marry.

Also in Ireland, was an amazing range of books and videos on both Michael Collins and associated subjects, many of which were, and are still, unavailable in England.

It was during those four years, after each visit to Ireland, my love for the country, its history, its people and their way of life, grew deeper. So too, did my fascination for Michael Collins – the more I learned about him, the more intriguing he became. Finally, in June 2000, I was offered a job in Dublin. I had achieved my ultimate dream, a chance to live and work in the country I had grown to love and felt totally at home in.

I quickly settled into my new life in Ireland and found myself, quite by chance, living in Howth, a peninsula north of Dublin Bay, about ten miles from the city centre. By sheer co-incidence, I later discovered, Howth was one of Michael Collins' favourite resorts in the Dublin area, Greystones at the southern end of the bay, being the other. It was to Howth that he used to escape for peace and quiet, during the height of the War of Independence. Perhaps the rugged cliffs and the cries of the wild seabirds, reminded him of his own beloved West Cork's coastline.

My research was now a lot easier and any spare time I had, was spent visiting various libraries, archives and museums, along with seeking out and meeting people, especially those whose family or friends had actually known Michael Collins. Gradually, Michael's true character and the kind of man he really was began to slowly unfold. The way he dressed and spoke to people, the practical and sometimes cruel schoolboy pranks he got up to, the music, books and plays he liked, even the kind of food and drink he enjoyed. I discovered he was passionately fond of Kerry Blue terriers and was in the habit of giving them as presents to his friends. Two, to his friend Harry Boland, when he went to America, and another to the socialite Hazel Lavery, whilst he was in London, after the Treaty talks in 1922.

I soon began to realise that all this information I was gathering could be the basis of an interesting and unusual book about Michael Collins, the man behind the mask. Not the soldier, statesman or guerrilla leader, of which numerous books have already been written, but the real, human, Michael Collins. One of my hobbies has always been photography, and over the past six years I have taken numerous photographs of various locations and buildings associated with him and his life. I

Michael's former quarters in Cathal Brugha Barracks (Portobello)

decided to include some of these in the book, and anyone who enjoys seeking out locations should find this of great interest.

I was very fortunate to gain access to many of Michael's safe-houses, offices, places of detention, as well as the more familiar locations such as his birthplace, schools, and other places of significance, many of which were already starting to disappear. I was very privileged to be given permission to photograph his quarters and office in what was Portobello, now Cathal Brugha Barracks, in Dublin, where, during July and August 1922, he was to spend the last few weeks of his life as Commander-in-Chief of the new Free State army.

Frongoch Prison camp in North Wales was also an interesting discovery, with its one surviving hut and old disused railway station. On 28 June 2002, eighty-six years after the prisoners first arrived at Frongoch, the local people of Bala, the nearest town to the camp, erected a commemorative plaque on the site of the old North Camp in memory of the 1,800 Irish prisoners held there after the Rising in 1916. However, I was unable to gain access to Stafford Gaol, where Michael along with the other rebels were first held in England, as it is still very much in use. The now derelict jail in Sligo, where Michael was imprisoned for three weeks was an interesting discovery, especially as I managed to find the actual cell he occupied, with its view of Knocknarea Mountain, which he commented about in his diary, written at the time.

During a visit to London about three years ago, I discovered the four houses

Barnsbury Hall

where Michael had lived with his older sister Hannie, from 1905 to 1916. On a more recent trip and after further research, I also found the locations of the City offices where he had worked as a young man, as well as various locations connected with him such as Barnsbury Hall in Islington, now a theatre, where he was sworn into the IRB (Irish Republican Brotherhood) in 1909, by Sam Maguire, after whom the All Ireland Gaelic Football Final cup, is named. Gaining access to 15 Cadogan Gardens, 22 Hans Place and 5 Cromwell Place, all locations associated with the Treaty talks in London during October to December 1921 was indeed a scoop, however, I was only able to photograph the hallways of the latter two.

I realised that through my research there may be one or two things I have discovered about Michael that might be controversial, especially in dealing with his relationships with women and particularly Kitty Kiernan. Here, I have tried to be factual and honest, as I have later in another chapter that deals with his frequent use of curses and strong language, which, for some, would not be the image they have of Michael Collins – he was a very human person!

I am greatly indebted to the many people who have helped me with my research. I was extremely honoured to have met and known Col Seán Clancy, who was born in 1901 and joined the Volunteers in 1917, and later the Free State army. He had worked with and knew Michael personally as a young man in Dublin during the War of Independence. He was also to stand beside him during the handover of Dublin Castle, in January 1922.

Also, the many members of the Collins family, especially grand-niece Mary Clare O'Malley and her family. Michael's grand-nieces Nora Owen and Mary Banotti, as well as Maureen Kirwin and Patsy Fallon, and his only surviving niece who remembered him as a child, Joan Bunworth. Grand-nephews Pol Ó Murchú and Tom Collins, whose help and encouragement will always be remembered. On his mother's side, the O'Briens, and a special thanks to Peg O'Brien-O'Driscoll and her brother Jim and family of Sams Cross, West Cork. Numerous people whose parents or grandparents, had helped, worked with or knew Michael, especially the O'Donovans of Rathgar, Dublin. The Kiernan family, Margot Gearty, Laurette Kiernan and Kitty's only surviving son, Michael Collins Cronin. My thanks also to Risteard Mulcahy whose father, Richard Mulcahy, knew Michael as a friend, as well as a fellow member of Dáil Éireann. They first met in Frongoch in 1916, and later, Richard became Minister for Defence and succeeded Michael as Commander-in-Chief of the army, after he was killed at Beál na mBláth in August 1922.

A special thanks to Molly O'Brien-Murphy, whose family sheltered Michael in Howth, during the Tan war, and to Joan Browne, whose grandmother was a first cousin of Michael's, living in Howth and later Dublin, during the early part of the twentieth century. Also, Brian Doyle, Margaret Connolly, Dave McKenna, Leslie Ó Laoi, together with the people of Howth, who have tried to help me with piecing together the jigsaw of Michael and his Howth connections. I am most indebted to Tim Pat Coogan, writer and historian, for his additional help and general advice. Also Meda Ryan, fellow author and biographer of Michael Collins, who kindly met me to share her experiences of writing and research.

To Dr Brendan Leigh-Doyle of Carlow, whose grandfather and family were closely connected to Michael throughout the War of Independence and its after-math. Also to Piaras O'Connor – whose two older brothers, Peadar and Seán, were members of Michael's Active Service Unit in Dublin and later, in 1922, the Free State army – who gave me amazing insight into the background of events during those times.

A big thank you as well to the numerous librarians, archivists, historians and particularly Comdt Victor Laing, of the Military Archives at Cathal Brugha Barracks, who was a great help encouraged me in the early days of my research, and to Capt. Dan Harvey at Collins Barrack, Cork.

My many friends and colleagues at Dáil Éireann, especially Maedhbh Mc-Namara, librarian and fellow author, for her invaluable advice on writing and get-ting a book published. Also Jim O'Keeffe, TD, for West Cork, and his family, Tim and Dolores Crowley, and the people in that part of Ireland, whose family or friends were either related or involved in events connected with Michael Collins and his times.

A big thank you to Catherine Ryan (the memory woman), antique and second-hand book seller, who lent me various books to assist with my research and to Gerry Donnelly who's knowledge of the Kerry Blue Terriers and Michael's interest in them, was extremely helpful. Also, the many other people too numerous to mention, who invited me into their homes, loaned me videos, books, letters, family mementos and every kind of useful information and source material. Most of all for their time and enthusiasm upon hearing of my project, especially the Lawlor brothers, Peader and Frank, whose father and uncles had known and worked for Michael Collins.

Last but not least, I should like to thank the late Michael Collins of Waterford, Johnny and Nancy's youngest son and Michael's nephew, who was not only in-strumental in helping me to move to Ireland, but inspired me to sit down and write this book about his favourite uncle. A big thank you to everyone.

1

MICHAEL COLLINS, LITTLE FELLOW, BIG FELLOW

Psychologists have often debated the concept of the charismatic leader, whether he or she becomes so by nature or nurture. Like most true talents, charisma must surely be innate, honed and improved by the learning process and experience, but a true gift of nature none the less.

There was one man who changed the course of Irish history, thrice blessed, not only charismatic, but also handsome and possessing a larger than life personality. He had a winning smile, warm personality, charmed women and inspired men, someone who in any walk of life would have been a success, earning him the popular title to which he was, and ever after, referred to by his followers and admirers. This was 'The Big Fellow', and that man was Michael Collins.

The Little Fellow

The 'Big Fellow' was once a 'Little Fellow', born in the early hours of the morning of Thursday 16 October 1890 at Woodfield, a small farm nestling in the hills of West Cork, about three miles from Clonakilty. The land had been in the Collins' family for seven generations. Michael was the youngest of eight children, three boys and five girls, born to Michael Collins, a farmer and his young wife Marianne (*nee* O'Brien) nearly forty years his junior.

Michael's father was sixty years old when he finally married, in 1876, Marianne his fatherless goddaughter, who lived with her brothers, sisters and elderly mother, at a farm in Sams Cross, a small hamlet about half a mile down the laneway from Woodfield.

Patsy Fallon, whose grandmother was Margaret Collins-O'Driscoll, Michael's oldest sister, gave me an interesting insight into Marianne's character. When she married Michael's father at twenty, she realised that due to lack of education she would have no other choice but to remain a farmer's wife for the rest of her days. This, however, prompted her to ensure that any daughters she had would receive educational opportunities equal to that of her sons. All five girls were to do very well, either as teachers or civil servants, or in Helena's case, joining a convent in England and becoming a nun.

Despite the difference in ages, the marriage was a happy one, and after a year, Margaret, the oldest was born in 1877. Then, with about a year and a half's gap between each child came John, Johanna (Hannie), Mary, Helena, Patrick and Kathleen (Katie), after which three years elapsed before the last child Michael was born. Michael senior was by now seventy-five years old but his powers, both intellectual and physical, were still undiminished.

Michael was only seven when his father died in March 1897 but those few years together made a great impression on the small boy. His father was particularly fond of his young namesake and helped instil into him his great love for old people, something Michael was to have all his life. Little Michael tried to help his father around the farm, and in turn, Michael senior told him legends and tragic tales of Ireland's history and quoted lines in praise of nationalism. He had, as a young man, joined the Fenian Brotherhood, later to become the IRB (Irish Republican Brotherhood), a secret society dedicated to bringing about Ireland's independence from Britain.

Many an evening Michael and his family would gather around the kitchen fire in the old farmhouse at Woodfield, to discuss O'Connell or Thomas Davis and the children soon became familiar with the rebel songs and poems of the era.

There had been a significant history of conflict in the area during 1798. The battle of Big Cross had taken place near Clonakilty, and a branch of the Collins' family, who lived next door to the farm at Woodfield, had suffered along with many other local families, at the hands of the militia combing the area for rebels.

It was also around this time that young Michael became friendly with James Santry, an old Fenian blacksmith, who had the forge at Lisavaird, another small village on the road between Clonakilty and Rosscarbery. The boy would spend many hours in the company of the old man, as he worked away in the forge, listening to his stories of the 1798 Rebellion and Father Murphy, and how he, himself, had made pikes for the 1848 and 1867 rebellions against the British.

No one outside the family was to have a more profound influence on the young Michael than James Santry. At the age of eight, he was to tell his brother, 'there is no man I have greater regard for. I have heard him speak of the Ireland he wished to see. When he struck the spark on the anvil, he struck the anvil in my heart. When I leave school, the only pursuit I want to engage in is the winning of the freedom of my country'.

Another person who was to have a great influence on the young Michael was his schoolmaster Denis Lyons, who also was an active member of the IRB. Although Michael was only four and a half when he first attended the local national school at Lisavaird he soon, under the influence of his teacher, developed a pride in being Irish and a keen sense of history and the wrong doings his country had suffered over the centuries under British rule.

Michael grew up in a very happy and loving environment. Although the family were not rich, they had a good standard of living and were self-sufficient. The Collins' were all hard workers but never hard drinkers. Michael was particularly loved and fussed over both by his mother and elder sisters. Hannie, who he later went to live with as a teenager in London, was to say 'We thought he had been invented for our special edification!' After his father died, Johnny, his oldest brother, took over running the farm as well as keeping a fatherly eye on the boy. His other brother, Patrick, decided quite early in life to go to America and was never to return to his native land.

Michael was a particularly bright child and many years later, when he had been smuggled in to the police barracks at Great Brunswick Street, Dublin (now Pearse Street) at the height of the War of Independence, to look through the files, he came across one on himself which described him as 'coming from a particularly brainy West Cork family'. Michael was thoroughly amused and he subsequently took great delight in quoting this to his pals.

Although Michael's father was a farmer, he was also a scholarly man and had learned from a wandering 'hedge' schoolmaster to speak French, Latin and Greek. He was also good at mathematics, widely read, and had an amazing memory, all abilities his youngest son possessed. Michael's mother Marianne, also encouraged her youngest son from an early age to read, and these numerous skills helped the thirteen year old Michael to progress from the local school at Lisavaird, to further his education at the National School in Clonakilty. Here he studied for the Post Office Boy Clerkship exam, which at the age of fifteen and a half, he passed with flying colours. He was offered a job in London, to work as a Boy Clerk in the Post Office Savings Bank in West Kensington, where his older sister Hannie was already working as a ledger clerk. In July 1906, Michael left home and his 'beloved' West Cork to join his sister in London. For the rest of his life Michael never lost his love for West Cork and often quoted 'Ye can take a man out of West Cork, but ye cannot take West Cork out of a man!'

He spent nearly ten years working and living in London and he had four different jobs. Each job helped lay the foundations for his various roles as Director of Organisation, Intelligence and Minister for Finance later on, during the War of Independence.

During those years in London Michael and Hannie lived at four different addresses. When Michael first joined Hannie in 1906, he shared her small bed-sit at 6 Minford Gardens, a late Victorian, four storey house in Shepherds Bush, just around the corner from the Post Office Savings Bank, where they were both working. By 1908, they managed to find a more spacious flat, this time above a bakery, at 11 Coleherne Terrace, now part of Brompton Road, which they occupied for five years until 1913. This second address has an interesting connection with my own life. For it was at 11 Coleherne Road, a five storey family house built in the 1870s, and later turned into five flats, that I too lived in London, from 1975 to 1981. No. 11 Coleherne Terrace is on the corner of Coleherne Road, now no longer a bakery

No. 11 Colherne Terrace

but an up-market café. Unfortunately, during the time I was living there, I had no idea of this intriguing link with Michael Collins.

As their landlord at 11 Coleherne Terrace decided to sell both his business and property in 1913, Michael and Hannie moved to another flat in Notting Hill at 28 Princes Road – a small artisan house built in the mid nineteenth century. Michael always had a fascination for the Notting Hill area, with G. K. Chesterton's *The Napoleon of Notting Hill* being one of his most read and treasured books.

Their move in early 1914 to 5 Netherwood Road, an early 1900s three-storey house, back in the Shepherd's Bush area, was to be Michael's last address in London. This was a substantial flat, above a dairy, comprising two bedrooms, a sitting-room, kitchen and bathroom (a great luxury to most working class people at the time). Michael returned to Ireland in early January 1916, although his sister I believe continued to live at their London flat until she retired from the post office in the 1940s.

This property is the only one of the four London homes that Michael and Hannie lived in, which is marked with a plaque. Unveiled by Clive Soley, MP, in July 1987, it only shows Michael's signature, his birth and death dates and that he resided there. There is no mention of who or what he was – perhaps this is a subject that Britain, even today, finds difficult to come to terms with.

While living in London, Michael was very involved with the Gaelic League, the Gaelic Athletic Association and joined Sinn Féin at their London Headquarters in Chancery Lane, close to where he was working in the City. In 1909, like his father, he also joined the IRB (Irish Republican Brotherhood) where he enjoyed rapid promotion from being on the local committee to becoming, in 1914, treasurer of the London and south-eastern area. It was at this juncture that he was involved with and helped organise the *Asgard* gun-running, at the small fishing village of Howth in County Dublin.

By 1916 his early interest in politics and Ireland's destiny as a young boy, began to bear fruit. In early January of that year, he left his job in the City of London and his sister Hannie, to return to Ireland. He settled in Dublin, joining the local Volunteers and was soon promoted to the rank of staff captain. April 1916 was to see Michael, as aide de camp to Joseph Plunkett, in the front line of the fighting at the General Post Office in Dublin, during what was to become known as the ill-fated Easter Rising.

The Big Fellow Again
The reference to being 'big' certainly was not directed at Michael's weight. Although reasonably tall, at five foot eleven inches, he kept relatively slim for most of his life, weighing around thirteen to fourteen stone. He did have a sweet tooth, and even with his tea or coffee, always accompanied it with two large spoonfuls of sugar. However, his love for cream buns, pancakes, etc., had very little effect of this vibrant, energetic young man, as he strode through the streets of London or Dub-

lin, bounded up stairs, taking in two or three at a time, or cycled at manic speed through the curfewed and often dangerous streets and alley ways of Dublin, during the height of the Irish War of Independence. Michael's sheer adrenaline alone would have kept him relatively slim, accompanied with the fact that he often had no idea when or where his next meal would be, and a hasty sandwich or bun, washed down with a mug of sweet tea, was sometimes all he would have to keep him going.

It was during the last year of his life, from around the time of the Truce in July 1921 that he finally began to put on weight, brought about by a complete change of lifestyle. He was no longer the man on the run, and was to spend those final months of his life in endless meetings, negotiations and, on the odd occasion, being a normal human being, socialising with his fiancée, Kitty Kiernan.

During and after the Treaty negotiations in London, he attended numerous lunches and dinner parties with the rich and famous of that era. It was around the end of 1921, that a colleague of his, Robert Brennan, who had worked for him on and off throughout the War of Independence, noticed that Michael's clothes were tighter fitting than usual. Brennan told Michael at the time 'You're getting fat' to which he replied 'I know I am!' Michael was to weigh nearly sixteen stone when he was killed a few months later in August 1922.

Michael, as a young man during the ten years he worked and lived in London, had always led a very active life, even although his jobs were of a desk bound, clerical nature. Soon after he first arrived in London, he became involved with the GAA and the London Irish Clubs. He was a great supporter of both hurling and Gaelic football, and as well as playing both games for a local team, the Geraldines based in Islington, North London, he was also to become their secretary. Along with this, Michael enjoyed athletics, and was to win a couple of medals for sprinting and the long jump.

Amongst his other activities in London at that time were visits to the local Irish ceilidhes, organised through the Gaelic League. Michael was a very social creature, as well as an excellent dancer, being very light on his feet, and was never short of female company to enjoy the evenings with.

After the surrender at the GPO in April 1916, Michael, along with a few hundred others, were transported back to England and imprisoned there for about nine months. They were first held at Stafford Jail but after a few weeks were transferred to Frongoch prison camp, near Bala, set in the beautiful countryside of North Wales. The internment camp had originally been a distillery but, at the commencement of the First World War, had been turned into a concentration camp for German prisoners. After the Rising in 1916, the British authorities decided to move the Germans and use Frongoch to accommodate some 1,800 less important Irish rebels. Michael was one of them. Many other Irish prisoners were not so lucky, such as De Valera and Harry Boland, who were incarcerated in Dartmoor Prison, surrounded by the bleak moors of Devonshire.

Old railway station at Frongoch. A small branch line built for a distillery – originally on the site of the prison camp – would have been used to convey the internees

The camp was divided into two – south and north – and Michael was based in the latter. Here, he soon became active in organising the local hurling and football matches between the two camps, and found the weekly twenty mile route marches through the wild and beautiful Welsh mountains most exhilarating, usually out-walking his guards. All this exercise, combined with a frugal diet, gave Michael little chance to put on any weight whilst being a guest of His Majesty.

At Frongoch, he was once again involved with the IRB and was soon elected Head Centre, or senior member, for the camp, later to be known as the 'University of Revolution'. Here, with his fellow inmates such as Richard Mulcahy, Seán Hales, and Gearóid O'Sullivan, Michael planned their next move in the fight for Ireland's freedom. They discussed the tactics of the Boers in South Africa, and realised their 'hit and run' ambush technique could also one day be used by Ireland, as a new method to fight a superior British army.

Michael resumed his study of the Gaelic language and was fascinated in hearing the local tradesmen and guards speaking in Welsh, a language not unlike Irish. He was amazed that the Welsh people, living so close to England, had managed to keep their native language alive over the centuries. He soon became friendly with a young sixteen-year-old local lad Robert Roberts, who helped at the camp's canteen/shop selling sweets, cigarettes, etc., to the internees. As the friendship grew, Roberts brought into the camp Welsh dictionaries and books on grammar, borrowed from the library, in nearby town of Bala, for Michael to study and compare the two ancient languages. Michael made quite an impression on the young lad especially after his 'mother' gave Roberts a tie-pin in the shape of a shamrock in-laid with green Connemara stone, for Robert's kindness to 'her' son, during his internment! Michael's mother by then had been dead nearly ten years, but it was a cunning way of winning over the lad's loyalty.

Interior of the only remaining wooden hut on the north camp site at Frongoch

Whilst being detained both at Stafford and Frongoch Michael's nickname, the 'Big Fellow', gained momentum. He was making his presence felt amongst fellow prisoners, whether they liked him or not, and was becoming recognised as a natural boss. As previously mentioned, he was very successful at sports, and was just beaten by the champion of Munster at a weight-throwing competition, by a few yards. He was tough, and any show of toughness in the camp called forth an answering toughness on his part. He gave any group he joined the feeling that something big and unusual had arrived amongst them. He could be a bully with his scowl, his fist-hammering on the table and his tornadoes of oaths and epithets. However, his fellow prisoners soon recognised that there was a warm, soft side to him and his reference to 'Those bloody lousers' was reserved to his equals in the movement and not subordinates.

Michael was certainly rumbustious and terribly noisy. As a fellow inmate, Desmond Ryan, observed in the yard at Frongoch: 'From a frenzied mass of swearing, struggling, perspiring players rolling and fighting over a ball – the description would fit a rugby maul rather than the Gaelic football occasion it was – he saw a wiry, dark-haired young man emerging, whose West Cork accent dominated the battle for the moment. He then went under and rose again and whooped and swore with tremendous vibrations of his accent before disappearing again'. After the game, he was told 'That's Mick Collins', although in late 1916, the name meant nothing to him.'

By Christmas 1916 the last of the internees, including Michael, were finally released from Frongoch. Michael, together with his cousin and fellow West Corkman, Gearóid O'Sullivan, who was later to become one of his closest associates, headed back to West Cork. However, his brief return to Woodfield was to be an unhappy one, with both his brother and sister-in-law ill, and his maternal grandmother recently dead. In fact Michael, according to the diary of Cornelius Connolly, a close friend of his during the War of Independence and Civil War, was to spend most of Christmas 1916 with Gearóid's family at their farm in Colnagrane, just outside of Skibbereen. After a month of kicking his heels and feeling bored, Michael decided to return to Dublin, and from then on, until the Truce in July 1921, his life became that of a man of action and on the run. His early years of sports and athletics stood him in good stead for those exhausting years ahead of him, organising and fighting, in what was to be know as Ireland's War of Independence.

Here was man with a price on his head, sleeping in different safe-houses most nights, cycling around the streets of Dublin on his old Lucania or Raleigh bicycle. During this period, he had many a narrow escape through skylights, over walls, hiding in cupboards or attics. He often worked a twenty-hour day, rising at dawn and rarely returning to his various beds before the early hours of the next day. A favourite saying of his was 'Oh, the hours wasted in sleep!'

Michael with his bicycle

All this was to come to an end after the Truce in July 1921. He gave up his bicycle and was usually driven, although quite a competent driver himself, either by Joe O'Reilly or Joe Hyland, to various meetings and appointments. From being Director of Intelligence, Minister of Finance, amongst other posts, he became in October 1921 one of the five Irish plenipotentiaries sent to London to negotiate the Treaty with the British Government, which took nearly two months to complete.

Then in early 1922, with the handing over by the British of twenty-six counties to the new Provisional Government, Michael was appointed its chairman. Once again, he was locked into endless meetings and negotiations. In July of that year, with the outbreak of Civil War, he left his cabinet position and became head of the newly formed Free State army as its Commander-in-Chief. He held this position for a mere six weeks before he was killed in Beál na mBláth on 22 August 1922, a few miles from where he was born in West Cork.

Michael in 1917

Sadly during those last few months of his life, Michael's health began to fail, due partly to stress but mainly total exhaustion, both mental and physical. Having spent five years on the run, he was to find, after signing the Treaty on 6 December 1921, not only a divided cabinet, but also many of his old friends, including Harry Boland, had turned against him. He feared a Civil War was looming and with a heavy heart, tried to find a compromise between the two sides.

He had for some time suffered from a stomach ulcer, which, during the last year of his life, frequently caused him a great deal of pain. The first time it manifested itself was after the famous Christmas Eve 1920 incident at the Gresham Hotel in O'Connell Street, Dublin. This was, and still is along with the Shelbourne, one of the most prestigious hotels in Dublin. Michael was hosting a dinner party that evening for some of his closest friends. Suddenly a group of Auxiliaries (ex-

British army officers that Churchill had sent over to Ireland to help the RIC) burst into the dining-room where the men had just finished their meal. Michael was singled out and taken to the hotel cloakroom, where he was searched at gun-point, his head held under a bright light by one of the soldiers, who was studying his features against an old photograph. Fortunately, luck, as always, was with him that night and Michael along with his friends were allowed to go free. After the incident, the somewhat traumatised Michael ordered another bottle of Jamesons – his favourite whiskey – the Auxiliaries having drunk the first one. The men spent the rest of the evening celebrating Michael's and their own lucky escape, and all getting extremely drunk, including Michael, something he rarely did. The following morning, Christmas day, found him suffering severely from his stomach ulcer and he spent the next few days of the festive season on a diet of curds and whey!

Physically, Michael was exceptionally strong, healthy and full of energy and even as a boy escaped most of the common ailments that children suffer from. In later years, he became more prone to coughs and cold, as his life on the run began to take its toll. On his last trip down to West Cork in August 1922, he was suffering not only from a particularly bad cold bordering on pleurisy, but also his stomach ulcer was playing up again. It is interesting to note Sir John Lavery's description of Michael, when he met him again in London during the Treaty negotiations in late 1921, to paint his portrait. He described Michael as 'a young Hercules, with a pasty face, sparkling eyes and a fascinating smile.' The 'pasty' face is often a sign of bad health, and it is quite possible that Michael, even then, in late 1921, was already suffering from a slow bleeding ulcer, causing him to become anaemic. After Michael was killed and his body was being embalmed at St Vincent's hospital in Dublin, the doctor, Oliver St John Gogarty commented that Michael's skin was like 'undiscoloured ivory', again rather unusual for a healthy, young man. The ulcer had plagued Michael for some years but during the last few months of his life, started to cause him a great deal of pain, aggravated no doubt by months of erratic living, stress and anxiety over the outcome of the Treaty and the threat of Civil War. I feel sure that the state of Michael's health on 22 August 1922, certainly did not help his judgement on that final, fatal evening in Beál na mBláth, when he shouted, 'Stop, and we'll fight them!'

2

A Handsome Minister of Finance

This is the description Harry Boland, his close friend and later rival in love, was to use when seeing Michael in the propaganda film promoting the setting up of the 'Dáil Loan' in 1919. The film was shown all over Ireland and in the United States during Harry's and De Valera's fund-raising tour there in 1919. Harry wrote to Michael from New York saying 'that film of yourself and Hegarty selling Bonds brought tears to my eyes. Gee boy, you're some movie actor. Nobody could resist buying a Bond and we have such a handsome Minister of Finance!'

Michael Collins was the classic 'tall, dark and handsome man', five feet eleven inches tall, broad shouldered and muscular, with a commanding physical presence and boundless vitality. His hair, tousled and thick, was in fact a mid brown, and not black as sometimes described. It had been fair as a child but darkened to brown when he was around twelve years old. His one mannerism was a frequent toss of his head, to shake back the dank mop of hair that fell across his brow.

His most distinctive feature were his eyes, deep set and wide apart. They were grey, flecked hazel, with long, dark eyelashes. Normally they twinkled with good humour but occasionally they would narrow, and their penetrating gaze could be either quite disconcerting or very captivating, depending on the circumstances.

His boyish face was oval and always clean shaven except for two occasions during 1921, when Michael grew a moustache. The first time was as form of dis-

guise from the British while electioneering for the Armagh constituency, which he won on the 24 May. He grew it again from around the time of the Truce, 11 July, up until the conclusion of the Treaty talks in December. This time it was partly to alter his appearance in case the Truce broke down and Ireland moved back into a war situation, but mainly to make him appear older than his thirty years. Of the five delegates sent to London in October 1921, Michael was the youngest by at least a decade.

Even in Stafford Prison and Frongoch, Michael contrived to have a good personal appearance, although when he was interned at the latter, he rarely bothered to wear a collar or tie, and wore old army boots, which he never cleaned. He was however essentially a clean-shirt man, always fastidiously neat and tidy, his face never showing a trace of 'blue-chin' or even the beginnings of a beard. For this most extraordinary effort of clean-liness in the conditions of internment, he became the butt, much to his annoyance, of the other internees, who invariably looked like brigands. 'D'you pull 'em out, Mick' they jeered at him, referring to his lack of hairy growth on face and chin. No doubt Michael had thought the matter over, coming to the conclusion to enforce a certain show of bombast on the other prisoners, many of whom, early on, came to know that lack of hairs on Michael's features, certainly did not mean a lack of strength.

A long, fine chiselled nose, below which was a well-arched firm mouth with a curling lip and a jaw prominent and determined. A gap between his front lower teeth could be seen when he laughed. When speaking or listening, he had a trick of jerk-ing his face around suddenly to the right or left of his shoulder – a peculiarly char-acteristic attitude. However, upon making some assertion that he expected to hear contradicted, or uttering a determination, he had a habit of thrusting out his chin in a peculiarly dogged manner.

It is interesting to note that throughout the period 1917 to 1922, Michael pre-sented himself as a prosperous businessman. He understood the simple psycho-logy of acting naturally and looking the part. He dressed smartly in line with his 'company director' image, and carrying his briefcase, would stride or cycle around the city, passing the time of day with who ever came his way, whether they were British soldiers, RIC or even the Auxiliaries! He soon learned that portraying himself as a 'clean collar and tie' man, was not the image usually associated with a terrorist. This was good psychology, as it exploited the natural human impulse to stereotype. It also made a good impression on the boys up from the country, who meeting him for the first time, found his businessman image helped to boost both their confi-dence and trust in him.

It was amazing how Michael, so charismatic and handsome, escaped being caught over those six years, although he did have some 'close shaves' as he used to say. Dublin in 2003 is still a small, friendly city but then, eighty-five years earlier, would have been a much smaller, closer knit community. I have often heard that when he made an appearance at a hotel or bar, heads would turn, especially the female ones. Perhaps he remembered what Joseph Mary Plunkett had told him back in 1916 'If you are on the run, forget you are on the run!' This, once again, showed Michael's excellent use of psychology, where the right body language under cer-tain circumstances, could be the best disguise of all.

Michael was always immaculately dressed and particularly neat and tidy in his habits. His suits were usually dark grey or navy, the trousers with a cross poc-ket, into which he frequently thrust his hand, accompanied either with a light rain-coat or in the winter, a dark wool top coat with a velvet collar. He was to buy him-self a new winter coat before venturing over to England in October 1921 for the Treaty talks, remembering that London, especially during that time of the year, could be extremely cold. Occasionally he wore a cap but usually a soft trilby, size seven, sometimes with a feather stuck jauntily in the headband. By the second decade of the twentieth century, trilbys, rather than bowler hats had started to be worn by the more fashion conscious middle classes, an image that Michael wanted to portray. It was said by people who knew him at the time, that he always dressed like an 'English' businessman.

Always having good dress sense, dapper rather than ostentatious, Michael was able to spend more on his clothes when he became a public figure from around July 1921. This can be borne out by a receipt from Kennedy & McSharry outfitters in Westmoreland Street, Dublin, which I came across during my research. Dated 7 February 1922, Michael had purchased amongst other items one pair of gloves costing £1.7s.6d., six silk handkerchiefs for £1.19s. and two pairs of pyjamas at £3. The total bill amounted to £9.18s.6d., which in 1922, was the equivalent to a months' wages for a working man.

I also discovered a letter written by Michael, when he was Commander in Chief, addressed to Messrs Callaghan & Co. Ltd. of Dame Street, Dublin, dated 5 August 1922, which again illustrates his concern in his appearance: 'I am sending back uniform to be pressed, to have pocket button put in tunic, and the belt hooks slightly lowered as arranged with Mr Lehane. It is absolutely necessary to have this attended to today as I must return the tunic sent yesterday – it is too tight, in the waist and neck. You did not send me a pair of leggings yesterday. You might also send me a few pairs of socks (some greenish colour) and the collars.'

The two personal items Michael normally carried with him were his Waterman fountain pen, kept in the pocket of his waistcoat, and up until around the time of the Treaty talks in London, a silver half hunter watch and chain. It was around then that he took to wearing a wristwatch, which can be seen clearly in the photos taken in London in late 1921 and in paintings of him by Sir John Lavery. This was another example of Michael being very fashion conscious and wanting to promote his image as a modern, successful businessman. He also bought a wristwatch for Kitty Kiernan, the young woman he met first in Co. Longford whilst campaigning for the 1917 by-election, and later had fallen helplessly in love with. On Saturday 8 October 1921, the day before Michael left for London, they became secretly engaged, and Michael presented her with the wristwatch, saying, 'She could listen to its tick and think of him twenty-four hours a day!'

He always wore leather shoes or boots, size nine, and these would be enhanced with a steel cap on the heel causing his footsteps to be heard echoing down the street, certainly not the custom of a man on the run. However, he did have a habit when leaving his numerous offices or safe-houses, of blowing his nose, to cover a good part of his face in case any spies or 'G' men were looking out for him. A 'G' man was a plain clothed detective working for the Dublin Metropolitan Police, 'A' to 'F' were the uniformed divisions.

At all of his various 'safe-houses', the womenfolk took care of his laundry. One such address was 44 Mountjoy Street, a stone's throw from Vaughan's Hotel in Dublin's inner northside, which was run by a Miss McCarthy from Kerry. Michael had lodged there having returned from Frongoch, but as things began to 'hot up' after 1919, it rapidly became unsafe for him to stay more than a couple of nights in one place. He had, however, during that time built up a good relationship with Miss McCarthy and continued to visit the house once a week, up until the Truce in 1921, to collect his laundry. He also used the laundry services of the prestigious Gresham Hotel in O'Connell Street, Dublin. Michael was always grateful to the many women who looked after him and helped maintain his smart businessman's image. He frequently left a ten-shilling note for the women who mended his socks, which at the time, when the average wage was around £2 a week, was very generous.

Ten years living and working in London had subtly refined Michael's West Cork brogue but in passion, anger or boisterous good spirits, this veneer of the metropolis would vanish and he would revert to the thick sounds of his native county. This burly, barrel-chested young man possessed a deep voice, described variously as gruff or gravely, a bear growl of a voice, yet it could become soft and husky when occasions demanded. It was a voice that readily betrayed the fire, the passion or the emotion of the speaker. He had a true Celtic temperament, a man who was easily moved to tears but with an inner strength not to mind showing his feelings.

Whilst discussing Michael's accent, I discovered the one word he could not pronounce properly was 'eggs', it always came out at 'oiges'. During the War of Independence, when the police and army were hunting down Michael, a suspect 'Michael' was often asked to say the word 'eggs'! How many ever passed the test will never be known.

It was Michael's custom in moments of relaxation to assume the accent, pronunciation and idiom of his native Cork, thereby lending additional point to his droll and witty remarks, descriptions and denunciations. As a rule, he spoke perfect English and his writings and speeches were unexceptionable but it was a kind of humorous affection with him among his intimate friends, to use words and pronunciations peculiar to West Cork. Irish words and ejaculations were mingled freely with his English and he was not very sparing in the use of expletives. However, when ever in the company of women, swearing was strictly forbidden. This rule was laid down by Michael and included not only him, but also any men working with him. In particular it concerned the small army of devoted women, secretaries, typist and couriers, who worked in the various offices around Dublin, set up to run his many diverse organisations. Seán Dowling, a close colleague of his around 1920–21, remembered an interesting anecdote in connection with Michael's swearing. Maureen Power, a friend of Dowling and also very involved with the movement, was attending a meeting, along with Seán Treacy and Michael Collins. Michael, forgetting Maureen's presence started going full pelt with the language (swearing). Treacy jumped up saying 'How dare you go on like that in front of a lady!' It stopped him, he recoiled at once and was most apologetic to both of them.

His laugh was not the deep guffaw which some considered a hearty laugh but more a high-pitched chuckle of intense appreciation. He had a keen sense of the ridiculous and a quickness of repartee in keeping with the rapidity of his mental process.

Signe Toksuig from Denmark married Francis Hackett, an Irishman, around 1910 and lived with her husband in Ireland until the late 1930s. Both were interested and involved with the political events taking place in the country during that period. Signe always kept a diary and this is her entry, for a day in early January 1922, recalling her personal impressions of Michael at a meeting held in Dáil Éireann, in the Round Room, where he was debating the Treaty:

> Michael Collins uses rather few gestures in speaking and those seem natural movements to emphasise what he says. He quite naturally tosses his head back a little to one side and thrust forward a decisive but not brutal jaw. One seldom sees such a blend of strength and intelligence as his face shows. The long narrow eyes look subtle, the wide firm mouth looks 'indomitable' as Griffith says. He is big and rather heavily built but he moves with amazing quickness, his nose is firmly aquiline, his chin strong, a sculptor has seen in his face a likeness, Caligula's. It is a Roman profile. When he speaks, he fully convinces one that he means it, means it without any bunk whatsoever. When he says 'For goodness sake don't afflict us with any more speeches' his 'for goodness sake' has all the vigorous sincerity of far stronger language of which by the way he is said to be exquisitely capable. When he spoke at the Sinn Féin election meeting of foolishly bringing about war with England, thus playing into the hands of the 'Morning Post mentality', he said 'There is no sense in thaht' and although God knows this does not look impressive in print, he says it in such a way that the blunt homely sentence carries more weight than a whole peroration.

Dr Oliver St John Gogarty, who had, at the turn of the century, been an acquaintance of James Joyce, was by 1922, one of Dublin's prominent surgeons, as well as a writer and nationalist sympathiser. He said 'Michael moved with the natural grace of a ballet dancer, holding himself erect and striding purposely, with a jaunty, slightly swaggering air.' Gogarty, a generous character, was also Michael's friend, and had given him a key to his house in Ely Place, just a stone's throw from St Stephen's Green, Dublin, to use as a safe-house, if the need arose. The same key was found later in Michael's pocket, after he was killed. Gogarty was also the doctor who undertook the post-mortem on Michael's body, the report of which has never been found, after it was brought back to Dublin from Cork in August 1922. Gogarty, together with Desmond Fitzgerald, supervised the embalmer, to prepare Michael's body for the public lying-in-state at Dublin's City Hall, and made some interesting personal comments about Michael, during the embalming. 'His skin was very smooth, like undiscoloured ivory and he had the most beautiful hands, like those of a woman'.

Gogarty's comment on Michael's hands being long and slender like those of a woman was borne out by a comment made to me recently by Piaras O'Connor, who many years ago met Joe Hyland, one of Michael's drivers. Joe had the leather gauntlets worn by Michael at Griffith's funeral. Piaras asked Joe if he could try them on but despite having normal sized hands for a man, found them an extremely tight fit!

Joe also told Piaras that if he had been driving on the evening of Tuesday 22 August 1922, in Beál na mBláth, on hearing Michael's orders to 'Stop and fight them', he would have put his foot down, ignoring Michael. Once out of danger Joe would have turned around to Michael and said 'Did you say something Mick?'

3

THE MOST HUMAN OF MEN

Like many giants of history, Michael had a contradictory character. He was a man whose mood could change in a matter of seconds from the light-hearted, happy go-lucky, to the grim, angry and impatient. He would unashamedly laugh or cry as the mood took him.

A fellow West Corkman, remembering Michael some twenty years after he had died, said the following: 'He is still the most vivid figure of our time, with his grin and snarl, and his imbecile practical jokes, yet at the same time studious, the most human of men, kind in his impetus way, hot tempered and passionate with his friendships. We can picture him always tensed for action with the brilliant face so mobile that it changed in an instant from fury to laughter, the lightning swing of the body and the gallant toss of the head. He grows on us by his weakness, he is the most human of heroes'.

At heart, he was the eternal optimist and would naturally look for the good in anyone. An example of this was his relationship with Cathal Brugha, another veteran of the 1916 Rising. Brugha became Minister for Defence in the cabinet of the Provisional Government and Michael being Director of Intelligence, theoretically took his orders from Brugha. However, as he was also Minister for Finance, Michael decided his two positions were of greater importance than Brugha's one. The two men were total opposites, and even before the Treaty, had difficulty seeing eye to eye about things, especially Michael's use of guerrilla warfare, and the hit and run tactics against the British that he masterminded during the War of Independence. Brugha was also very anti-IRB and wanted nothing to do with the organisation. In November 1921, during the Treaty talks in London, Michael wrote to a friend about Brugha and it illustrates his kind-heartedness and generous spirit:

> I have often said that Brugha commanded respect and I still say the same, I respect a fighter and B. is one. Only he is misguided. Yet, even in enmity he is capable of sincerity, which is more than I can say of the others.

They were even more divided after the ratification of the Treaty in early 1922, and their clash of personalities was one of the many factors that led up to the disastrous Civil War. However right up to Brugha's death in July 1922, Michael was never to have a bad word said against him.

However, Michael did not suffer fools and could be extremely impatient, abrupt and stern with those who did not carry out his orders, even if they happened to be very good friends of his He had no time for explanations and would tell people, usually with a few oaths thrown in for good measure, just what he thought of them.

A classic example of this happened to Batt O'Connor one of his oldest and most loyal of friends, his home in Brendan Road being one of Michael's safest of safe-houses. The two men spent many an evening socialising and enjoying an odd drink together and Batt's wife and children were in many ways, Michael's extended family. However, there was the 'other' Michael that Batt was to recall in his book *With Michael Collins in the Fight for Irish Independence*. This is a brief extract of an event that took place in the Mespil Road office around 1920:

> During business hours he could be abrupt and stern in his manner. He had no patience for excuses for failure to carry out an order and would waste no time listening to explanations.
>
> We had run out of moulders sand and hard coke for one of our small bomb factories, and he had sent for me and told me to procure a ton of this special coke. I spent two days trying to get it, but discovered that it could only be sold to those carrying on a legitimate foundry trade. I had not means of proving that I was carrying on such a business.
>
> I went to Michael and began explaining the situation to him but I had hardly uttered half a sentence before he snapped out, 'Have you got it, or have you not got it? If you haven't got it, don't mind the excuses, but go and get it!'
>
> I was standing beside his desk, and putting down his head, he resumed his writing, with an air of dismissing me.
>
> 'Listen to me a moment Michael. Though I have not been able to buy it, if you can wait till Saturday I can commandeer it.'
>
> 'That is all I want Batt.' He is now looking up at me again. 'What are you wasting my time for? Go and commandeer it!' he ordered impatiently.

Underneath this sternness, however Michael was the most sensitive, tender and caring of men. His friends remembered that at heart he was the 'softest creation in the world' who loved old people, children and mothers and wept for the troubles of his friends. Even when he was busiest he never failed to visit sick friends or their relatives, or to pay the doctor's bill if it was necessary. He remembered all his friends in prison and the individual little delicacies they liked.

His sensitivity also included his respect for birds and animals. As a small boy he used to keep secret the birds' nests he found, even from his family or closest friends, in case they might disturb or steal the eggs. He would say triumphantly to his sisters, once the birds had flown away and the nests empty 'every one of them has flown away and the world is full of small birdeens.'

There are many interesting insights into Michael's vibrant and lively personality remembered by contemporaries. One such friend and later the first person to write a biography on Michael in 1926 was Piaras Béaslaí. He draws a picture of a typical night in Vaughan's Hotel, which was on the quiet side of Rutland Square, now Parnell Square. Here, it was a custom for groups of men from different parts of the country to assemble to meet the 'Big Fellow' as he was known as:

> The door swings open and Mick strides rapidly into the room. He looks around and all the men at the back rise and make a gesture to attract his attention. He scans them all rapidly, selects one, beckons to him and calls him aside. In about three minutes he has

Vaughan's Hotel

got the gist of the man's business, made a decision and scribbled a line on a sheet which he tears out of his notebook and places in his sock.

Then he calls to the next man and quickly grasps his problem. He makes an appointment for that man at a certain spot, at a certain hour next day – and woe betide that man if he comes a minute late!

With amazing speed, he disposes of all the problems and sends the men away contented. So thoroughly does he enter into each matter that each man leaves with the impression that only his worries are Collins' great concern ...

When he joins the regular frequenters of the place, his senior colleagues and aids at the table, he does not sit down first. His restless energy finds vent in various sudden movements which a chair would hamper.

His face continually changes its expression as he speaks or listens. He looks now grim, now jovial, now angrily impatient, now deadly serious, now impishly mischievous. When he encounters serious opposition, he thrusts out his chin doggedly and turns his head round until it is nearly in line with his shoulder.

Frank Thornton, one of his most trusted intelligence officers, arrives with a report of enemy activity and Collins goes aside to discuss the matter with him, along with Tobin and Cullen, who were also part of his intelligence network, and quickly determines what is to be done. Collins returns and announces he will stay in the hotel for the night. He asks to be called at seven in the morning. Gearóid O'Sullivan and Seán Ó Muirthile are also staying, and when Collins rises in the morning and finds they are still asleep in bed, he enters their room to waken them with a fire extinguisher!

Another friend and colleague, although after the Treaty, an opponent of Michael's, was Tom Barry, the hero of the Crossbarry and Kilmichael ambushes in West Cork during the War of Independence. Michael held him in high regard after the events, summoned him to GHQ in Dublin, and met him in his role as Director of Intelligence. Barry's equally high opinion of Michael shines through what he wrote of the visit:

The outstanding figure in all GHQ was Michael Collins, Director of Intelligence. This man was, without a shadow of a doubt, the effective driving force and backbone at GHQ of the armed action of the nation. A tireless, ruthless, dominating man of great capacities, he worked like a Trojan in innumerable capacities to defeat the enemy.

Barry saw Michael arriving at Vaughan's Hotel one evening around 6.30. He remembered Collins was swallowing his tea and then interviewing officers from the five country units, advising, encouraging or reprimanding. To one officer from a particular inefficient unit who asked for arms, Collins, with a scowl on his face, his hands deep in his pockets, his right foot pawing the ground shot back 'What the hell does a lot of lousers like ye want arms for? Ye have rifles and revolvers galore but ye have never used them. A single bowsy Black and Tan is walking around your area for six months, terrorising and shooting people and ye are afraid to tackle him. Get the hell out of this and don't come back until ye have done some fighting!'

Ernie O'Malley, on the Republican side after the Treaty paints this vivid word picture of his first meeting in 1918 with Michael at his Bachelors Walk office – at the time O'Malley was an up and coming Volunteer officer:

He was pacing up and down. We shook hands. He jerked his head to a chair to indicate that I should sit, he took a chair which he tilted back against the wall. On the shelves were green membership cards, heaps of *The Irish Volunteer Handbook*, and stacks of white copies of the organisation scheme. Behind his desk was a large map of Ireland marked with broad red streaks radiating out of Dublin. He was tall, his shoulders broad, his energy showed through rapid movement. A curving bunch of hair fell on his forehead, he tossed it back with a vigorous head twist. 'I'm sending you to Offaly,' he said. 'I want you to organise a brigade in the country ...'

He had a strong, singing Cork accent, his grey eyes studied me fixedly. He pointed out companies on a map and mentioned officers' names. 'It looks like conscription,' he said. 'That will make some slackers wake up'. He pointed out communication routes on the wall map. I was to improve and keep them tested by dispatch riders. He gave me a bundle of organisation schemes, instructions for the preparation of emergency rations, lists of equipment that could be made locally. 'Read that and see what you think of it'. He handed me notes on the destruction of railways, bridges and engines with or without explosives. It was signed by the Director of Engineering. He crossed to the window whilst I read. 'My bail is up,' he said, 'they're looking for me now.' 'They' meant the G men ...' Collins laughed. 'Good luck,' he said and shook hands.

Ladder leading to trap door in
Vaughan's Hotel – used by Michael
Collins as a means of escape

Another incident that Ernie O'Malley remembered was during an investigation conducted by Michael, of an IRA raid of arms from the British army around the period of the Truce:

> Coming over to where the men suspected of the raid stood, Collins planted his legs apart and thrust his head forward. 'Some of ye bloody fellows know about this. The rifles did not walk away. Negotiations in London will be held up over a few rifles. The British will say we have broken faith.' He tossed his hair back from his forehead with a shake of his head. 'Come on, by Christ and answer the question I ask.' His voice became threatening. 'We are not going to let ye get away with those lousy rifles.' He put his hands deep in his trouser pockets, lifted himself a little on his feet, came back again on his heels, then turned abruptly, walked out and banged the door.

No. 1 Brendan Road and No. 16 Airfield Road – Michael's two main safe-houses

4

MICHAEL, FIRST AND LAST A BUSINESSMAN

Michael was a businessman first and foremost, and very methodical in all he dealt with. Whatever sort of night he had passed, sharp at 9 o'clock he either cycled or strode down the street to one of his many offices scattered across the city of Dublin. These were a variety of temporary premises, serving many functions, finance, intelligence, propaganda, etc., necessary for a man constantly being pursued. Whoever was working as his secretary at the time, would have laid out his correspondence, stamped with the day's date and pinned to the envelopes. Michael would then go through it all with a coloured pencil, usually red, marking on each letter by numbers the different subjects to be dealt with, in order of importance. He normally always used a fountain pen and abhorred pencils, which he rarely used except for marking letters, unless in an emergency. He would be offended if anyone dared to write to him using a pencil, but a far worse offence would be for someone to use a rubber stamp, rather than a 'live' signature. After the typist arrived with the previous day's letters for signing, Michael would then dictate the replies to that day's correspondence. In each of his offices, he kept files in which every detail of his work was recorded. To those around him it was a constant invitation to disaster, even the capture of one file into the wrong hands could have meant the end of months of hard work in the fight for independence, but even worse, the end of his and his colleagues' lives.

As Michael dashed from one office to another, he carried little with him except sometimes, if on foot, his briefcase to fit his businessman image. More often, he would jump onto his old Raleigh bicycle, which clanked alarmingly as he sped around the streets of Dublin. One item he always carried with him, was his small black appointments diary, any other information that he needed at the time, would be scribbled on a piece of paper and tucked inside his sock. If either the police or the soldiers stopped him, this would be the last place they would think of searching.

It was essential that Michael ran a 'tight ship' in his various offices and had a strict rule for punctuality. Anyone arriving a second late would be greeted by him at the door, swinging his half-hunter pocket watch and glowering at them furiously.

Michael ran this vast organisation for raising loans, infiltrating arms and the enemy's secret service, as a business enterprise, with his staff at each office working fixed hours, as if they were employees at a local solicitors or bank. Of course, they were all hand-picked and loyal to him and the cause. Joe O'Reilly, from Bantry in West Cork, his most trusted secretary, as well as messenger boy, nurse, driver and confidant, worked for Michael from early 1917 until his death in 1922. Michael found Joe wandering along a street in Dublin, unemployed since his release from Frongoch in late 1916. Having been friends since they first met in London around 1910, Michael immediately offered him a job in his organisation and Joe devoted himself entirely to his boss and the cause for the next six years. After Michael's death, Joe became ADC to President Cosgrave and later held a good position in the Board of Works. He later married and had one daughter. Sadly, Joe died relatively young of cancer during the 1940s and now lies a few yards from where his boss, friend and fellow West Corkman is buried in Glasnevin Cemetery, Dublin.

Sinead Mason was another of Michael's personal and long-serving secretaries. She too was devoted and very loyal to the cause, her work and to him. He, in return, had complete confidence in her. Being his personal secretary, similar to Joe, she also worked long hours, travelled to various venues and often undertook dangerous tasks and, like Joe, continued to work for Michael up until his death, as his secretary at Portobello Barracks when he became Commander-in-Chief in July 1922.

Even as young as fourteen, whilst Michael was attending classes at the National School in Clonakilty, he began to develop secretarial skills. As the school was about four miles from where he lived in Woodfield, Michael used to lodge during the week with his eldest sister Margaret and her husband Patrick O'Driscoll, proprietor and chief reporter for a local paper *The West Cork People* in Clonakilty. Patrick decided to make use of his young brother-in-law and sent Michael out on assignments covering topical events such as weddings, football matches, etc. This gave him the opportunity to report facts with the minimum of words and to use a typewriter, skills which would prove very beneficial in later life.

However, it was Michael's ten years working in London from 1906 to 1916 that laid the foundation of his business and organisational skills. Having passed his Civil Service examination at fifteen, he went straight to London working for the Post Office Savings Bank in West Kensington as a boy clerk.

In 1910, he resigned from the post office and went to work for Horne & Company, stockbrokers in the City, where he was placed in charge of the messengers. He then went on to become a clerk at the Board of Trade in Whitehall, shortly after the outbreak of the First World War, and finally, in May 1915, went back to the City to work for an American company, The Morgan Guaranty Trust. One of the reasons Michael had chosen to work for an American company was, that around this time, he had been toying with the idea of joining his older brother Patrick in America, who had by then joined the Chicago police department. Due to the heavy losses on the western front, there was talk of conscription and young Michael had no desire to be in the British army and used as cannon fodder in Flanders. However, fighting for Ireland was another issue, and when he handed in his notice in January 1916 to return to Ireland, he told his employers that he was going to join a local regiment in Dublin. They, thinking he was about to join a British unit based in Dublin, gave him an extra week's salary, which he immediately donated to the IRB.

A few months earlier his boss, Mr Brown, had said to Michael 'Collins, its men like you that should be at the front. We need leaders like you. The bloody Germans are giving us extreme difficulties out there. I'll tell you what Collins, the night you sign up I'll give you a fiver, to go out and celebrate with your friends.' Later when he did 'sign up', Michael told his boss 'I'm joining up Mr Brown, I'm ready for the fight.' His boss, true to his word, gave Michael the fiver and he along with his pals, including his cousin Gearóid O'Sullivan, had a great night out on the town.

Whilst living in London he enrolled at King's College, to attend evening classes, in what is now known as creative writing. Also, when he was nineteen, Michael thought of joining the newly formed Customs and Excise Service. This required passing the Civil Service Exam, covering such subjects as accountancy, taxation, commercial law and economics, all of which he undertook to study and were all to prove very useful a few years later.

Obviously, Michael had a natural talent of all things financial. Even before he left London in 1916 barely twenty-five, he had become treasurer for both the IRB in London and the south of England, as well as for the London Branch of the GAA. A few years later, he was to sum up his career thus:

> The trade I know best is the financial trade, but from study and observation I have acquired a wide knowledge of social and economic conditions and have specially studied the building trade and unskilled labour. Proficient in typewriting, but have never tested speed. Thorough knowledge of double-entry system and well used to making trial balances and balance sheets.

All these skills enabled Michael the deskman, administrator and chief-of-staff, to successfully organise the campaign against the British Intelligence system during the War of Independence and later, in early 1922, to set up the new Irish Free State.

While undeniably he was a brilliant soldier, it is very unlikely that he ever killed anyone himself, recruiting others to do that. His role was more a paper-shuffling bureaucrat, than a gunman. Even at the GPO in 1916 he was aide de camp to Joseph Plunkett, and therefore in an administrative role. The only other time he was a soldier in uniform, was during the last six weeks of his life as Commander-in-Chief of the new Free State army, and it was at the ambush in Beál na mBláth that Michael took the fatal decision, countermanding Dalton's wise order to 'drive like hell' by shouting 'Stop, and we'll fight them'. It was possibly the first time Michael ever held a rifle with the intention of killing someone since his involvement at the GPO, and this lack of combat experience probably cost him his life.

Another interesting but little known venture of Michael's whilst living and working in London as a young man, was to attend voice-training classes, given by an actor, to enable him to learn how to throw his voice and address public meetings. This was to prove extremely useful later on and can be seen to full effect if one studies old newsreel footage of Michael addressing the crowds on various occasions. In fact, he was very alert to PR and quite theatrical and image conscious. His sheer physical energy and use of body language as he powerfully delivers his message, is quite remarkable. He did not fake Collins, he projected Collins, the real Collins, not only to his immediate audience, but also to the world at large.

Michael Collins as Commander-in-Chief of the army

5

The Man of Destiny

During the ten years he lived in London, Michael like his sister Hannie became an avid theatre-goer. George Bernard Shaw's play *The Man of Destiny*, based on the life of Napoleon, inspired the young Michael, to the point of copying out passages from the play and carrying them around in his wallet. He was fascinated by the life and deeds of this great soldier and empire builder, and perhaps subconsciously modelled himself on him.

Sir James Barrie's *Peter Pan* was another character, although this time fictitious, who Michael felt akin to. The name Peter Pan conjures up the image of a man who throughout his life retains his youthful features and good looks, something Michael certainly did during his brief life. Barrie had known the Davies boys, nephews of Crompton Llewelyn Davies, who along with his Irish wife Moya, were friends of Hannie, Michael's sister, and later around 1910, of Michael himself. The friendship evolved through their mutual interest in Irish culture, but more particularly, their membership of the Gaelic League in London. Barrie based his *Peter Pan* character on one of the Davies boys, also a Michael, who had drowned tragically, whilst studying at Oxford. At the time of the accident, Michael had a premonition that his life too would be short, and actually commented on this in a letter to Moya. As a point of interest Peter Scott, son of the famous Antarctic explorer Robert Falcon Scott, was also named after the character *Peter Pan*. Around the time young Peter was born 1910, Barrie was a very good friend of Robert Scott and his wife.

The Royal Court, or The Court as it was known at the time, in Sloane Square, Chelsea, was Michael and Hannie's favourite theatre in London. It was, and still is, associated with plays by Irish writers. Another London theatre frequented by Michael as a young man was the Coronet and he was often to be found in the gallery, especially if the Manchester Repertory Company were in town. Michael's love for the theatre continued all through his life, even during the height of the War of Independence. When time allowed him a free evening, he would frequent the Dublin theatres, often alone, perhaps to give himself a break from the horrors of everyday life in the war-torn capital. Michael was a regular visitor to the Abbey in Dublin's city centre and one night word was received that the place was surrounded by Black and Tans, who wanted to catch him dead or alive. Nellie Bushell, a member of Michael's ASU also worked at the Abbey as an usherette and upon hearing of the intended raid, calmly walked down to the stalls where Michael was sitting and whispered into his ear. Nellie then quietly led him to a backstage door and the elusive Michael was out like a flash into the laneway, just as the armed Black and Tans burst into the theatre and ordered all the lights be switched on, so they could scrutinise the audience. After the soldiers had left, empty handed, Michael slipped back in and enjoyed the rest of the play. Upon his return to London in the autumn of 1921, during the Treaty negotiations, he revisited the theatres again, especially his old haunt, the Royal Court, this time only a five-minute walk from his head-quarters at 15 Cadogan Gardens. Once again, he would escort his sister Hannie, who was still living in West Kensington, to a play. On other occasions he might accompany the Laverys, or the Llewelyn Davies', old friends as well as fellow lovers of the theatre.

Michael was throughout his life a great reader. His love of books first began when the family moved, in 1900, into their new home, a large house erected next to the old farm in Woodfield, where he was born. It was here that Michael, just ten years old, had his own bedroom for the first time. It was sparsely furnished from choice, his sole luxury was a little bookcase containing, for such a young boy, an amazing range of reading matter. There were books about his great heroes Wolfe Tone and Robert Emmet, martyrs of the Rebellions of 1798 and 1803; the writings of Thomas Davis, which left an indelible mark on his political philosophy; the poetry and essays of the Sullivan Brothers, which included 'God Save Ireland' the Fenian anthem; the patriotic novels of Banim, Kickham and O'Donovan Rossa's autobiographical *Prison Life*, together with others of a similar political theme. Alongside these were also the novels of Scott, Dickens and Thackeray, as well as Shakespeare and the poems of Thomas Moore.

In 1906 when Michael as a young man of fifteen went to work in London, his sister Hannie also had a great influence on his choice of reading matter, recommending such contemporary writers as Arnold Bennett, G. K. Chesterton, H. G. Wells, Conrad and Conan Doyle. It has been said that during the War of Independence, his use of young people as agents, go-betweens and messengers was initiated by his reading of Sherlock Holmes and the Baker Street Irregulars. He was also particularly fond of the works of Thomas Hardy, the tragic *Jude, the Obscure*, strangely being amongst his preferences. Along side these English writers, he also enjoyed reading the works of his fellow countrymen such as Oscar Wilde, Yeats, Stephens and Pádraig Colum.

Michael was to dabble in poetry and especially during his internment in Frongoch, would compose the odd poem to his girlfriend at that time, Susan Killeen. As his friendship with Kitty Kiernan developed into a more passionate affair, he introduced her to poetry and would write out lines for her to memorise during his absence, and have her recite them on his return visit. He even dashed off the odd line to Hazel Lavery, during the Treaty and post-Treaty visits to London in 1921–22, although I feel this was more done in fun than sincerity.

Poetry revealed the more gentle and often unknown side of Michael's nature, a part of him that is rarely discussed or even acknowledged. His poems, although simple and 'old-fashioned' were also quite romantic, which at heart he really was. He had grown up in a household dominated by women and throughout his life, he had a great respect and love for them. From his early days in London, his girl-friends were usually fellow Irish girls who he worked with or got to know at the ceilidhes and other social events run by the local Gaelic League or Irish clubs in the city. This romantic and rather intriguing side of Michael's character I will deal with separately, but here are four poems of his, the earlier two dedicated to Susan Killeen, his girlfriend during the 1916 era. The first was most likely written for her around St Valentine's Day, and the second composed at Frongoch Interment Camp:

> *Your smiling eyes and shining face,*
> *My arm around you to embrace,*
> *At times I wander in my thoughts,*
> *And come to rest in a cool green shade,*
> *It's there I imagine you sleeping sound,*
> *And lilacs growing all around.*
>
> *To awaken you is just a kiss away,*
> *And in my arms to rock and sway,*
> *In all sincerely I want to say,*
> *Be my valentine for just one day.*
> *Whenever you need me in gloom or cheer,*
> *You can be rest assured I'll always be near,*
> *With this line to be my second best*
> *My love for you in a die to be caste.*

> *I've run the outlaw's brief career,*
> *And borne his load of ill,*
> *His troubled rest and waking fear,*
> *With fixed sustaining will,*
> *And should his last dread chance befall,*
> *E'en that would welcome be,*
> *In death I'd love thee more than all.*
> *A Chushla gheal mo chroidhe.*

Michael's interest in poetry writing stayed with him throughout his short and turbulent life. During the Treaty negotiations and its aftermath in 1921–22, he was to renew his friendship with the Laverys. Moya Llewelyn Davies, along with her husband Crompton, had been friends of the Laverys for some time, and introduced Michael and his sister Hannie to them in London, around 1913. Hazel Lavery, wife of Sir John Lavery the painter, was a very beautiful and charismatic woman, and it would not have been difficult for any man to fall under her spell. It was rumoured at the time of the Treaty negotiations that Michael and Hazel were having an affair but it was more likely an older woman's infatuation for a younger man. Here are two poems written by Michael to Hazel around the spring of 1922. Michael had a very mischievous side to his nature and loved to wind people up, especially beautiful aristocratic women! I feel these two poems would have been written rather 'tongue in cheek':

Oh! Hazel, Hazel Lavery,
What is your charm Oh! say?
Like subtle Scottish Mary,
You take my heart away.
Not by your wit or beauty,
Nor your delicate sad grace,
Nor the golden eyes of wonder,
In the flower that is your face.

Cucugan I call thee,
Cucugan the dove,
Because of thine eyes and the voice that I love.
Cucugan I call thee,
Has thou no fear, little bird, little love,
I am the eagle and thou art a dove.
Hast thou no fear of me?
Wild is my nest in the mountain above,
Wilt thou fly there with me lovely white dove,
Shall my wings carry thee?

This second poem dedicated to Hazel, was written just a few weeks before Michael was killed in August 1922. Michael, busier than ever, was unable to find the time to write long letters to Kitty Kiernan but found time to write poetry to Hazel.

'The banks of my own lovely Lee' was Michael's, and Cork's, national anthem. This patriotic ballad would have also brought back happy childhood memories for Michael, especially the first two verses:

How oft' do my thoughts in their fancy take flight
To the home of my childhood away;
To the days when each patriot's vision seemed bright
Ere I dreamed that those joys should decay;
When my heart was as light as the wild winds that blow
Down the Mardyke through each elm tree,
Where we sported and played 'neath each green leafy shade,
On the banks of my own lovely Lee.

And then in the springtime of laughter and song
Can I ever forget those sweet hours;
With the friends of my youth, as we rambled along,
'Mongst the green mossy banks and wild flowers;
Then too, when the evening sun sinking to rest,
Shed its golden light over the sea,
The maid with her lover the wild daisies pressed,
On the banks of my own lovely Lee.

In Michael's mind it was not the banks of the river Lee, but the banks of the broad flowing stream the Owenahincha, a tributary of the Argideen, running through the valley between Woodfield and the foothills of Knockfeen, on its way down to Rosscarbery and the Atlantic ocean, that crashes against the wild West Cork coastline. It too, had mossy banks, wild flowers and green leafy shades, where the little fellow would have sported and played, catching eels and playing with his siblings and friends.

It was Michael, whistling this, his favourite tune, which helped his cousin Nancy O'Brien to identify him amongst the crowds of prisoners, after the Easter Rising in April 1916. Nancy had decided not to visit her family in West Cork that Easter, due, most likely, to her concern for her cousin and his involvement with the Rebellion. Michael had taken her into his confidence a few days earlier and discussed the proposed Rising. Instead, she decided to stay with friends in Howth and had watched with horror from Howth Head as the fires spread across Dublin during that fateful week. After the surrender five days later, she heard the surviving rebels, including Michael, hopefully, had been rounded up and kept overnight in the grounds of the Rotunda Hospital, a short distance from the now burnt out shell of the GPO. They were then transferred to Richmond Barracks where the British army, along with the detectives from Dublin Castle, segregated the ring-leaders and had them taken to Kilmainham Jail, where they were subsequently executed. Nancy, wanting to reassure herself that her young cousin was alive and well, decided to risk returning to the war-torn city, hoping to seek him out. She heard that the rest of the prisoners, including Michael, who had escaped Kilmainham and death, were being transferred to English jails. Nancy finally caught up with him as he and the rest of the Volunteers were being marched down to Alexandra Basin on the quays en route to the awaiting cattle ships that would transport them across to England. Through all the dejection and despondency of the captives, she heard the familiar whistle of Michael's favourite anthem 'On the banks of my own lovely Lee', and found him surprisingly, full of the joys of spring, his mind already forming future plans to continue the fight for independence. Michael putting his arm around her said, 'Come here Nancy girl, where can you do better conceptual thinking that in the grounds of the Rotunda Maternity Hospital!'

Because of the demands on his time and the incredible volume of work he undertook each day during the period 1917 to 1921, Michael had little opportunity to attend social events. On the rare occasions that he did attend a party, the fellow guests were unlikely to forget the occurrence. They would hear his laugh at the door as he bounded into the room. For the short while he was there, the company would be animated with his overcharged vitality. He was always the life and soul of any gathering, each guest wanting to have a word with him. When he had left, peace and normality returned, the flattened cushions where he had hurled himself, remaining the only evidence of his rumbustious presence.

Even as a small boy, Michael loved music, although, like his father before him, he was not a particularly good singer. When the Collins family gathered around the kitchen fire at the old farm in Woodfield on a cold winter's evening, to sing, recite poetry or tell a story, Michael often chose the old ballad 'Deep in Canadian Woods'. Michael, by his own admission, was an indifferent singer, but loved the old ballads and songs, especially those of Thomas Moore and Michael O'Rahilly, the latter who fought and died in the Rising of 1916.

During the War of Independence he would, in his rare moments of relaxation, ask Joe O'Reilly to sing for him. Eileen O'Connor, Batt's daughter remembered the Christmas of 1919, when Michael and Joe were staying with the family at Brendan Road, in the Donnybrook area of Dublin. Michael was particularly fond of 'The Foggy Dew', a song recently composed about the Easter Rising and persuaded Joe, who had a very good voice, to sing it for them. 'The West Awake' was another patriotic tune he particularly enjoyed hearing.

Possessing such a phenomenal memory, Michael knew the tunes and words of nearly one hundred ballads. As his romance with Kitty Kiernan blossomed, he would stay with her and the family at their hotel The Greville Arms in Granard, Co. Longford as often as was possible. There, assembled around the piano, Kitty or one of her equally musically talented sisters would sing the 'Londonderry Air' or 'Danny Boy' as it is also known, another of Michael's favourite melodies. The words to this melancholy song were to prove quite prophetic to Kitty within a few years. Another favourite was 'Bheirmeo' or 'The Eriskay Love Lilt'.

Another poem he was fond of was 'Old Skibbereen', which he had learned as a boy from his maternal grandmother. Skibbereen, a market town about twenty miles west of Clonakilty in West Cork and its surrounding countryside, had seen some of the worst evictions carried out by Protestant landlords and subsequent mass emigration of its local Catholic population during the nineteenth century. The area was also severely hit by the Great Famine in the mid 1840s. 'Old Skibbereen' recalled those tragic events and Michael's widowed grandmother, who came to

Greville Arms Hotel in Granard

live with the family in Woodfield when he was a boy, personally remembered and had survived those dreadful times. She was to relate first hand to her grandson Michael, stories of that terrible period in Irish history.

At social gatherings, as was customary at the time, people would get up and sing a song, play a tune, or recite their favourite poem or section of prose. Michael, usually with great gusto and appropriate gesture, would stand up and recite his 'party piece', the poem 'The Fighting Race' written by an Irishman Joseph Clarke about the Spanish-American War of 1898. The line 'When Michael, the Irish Arch-angel, stands' would always bring a twinkle into Michael's eyes and a smile to his lips:

> Read out the name!' and Burke sat back,
> And Kelly drooped his head.
> While Shea – they called him Scholar Jack –
> Went down the list of the dead.
> Officers, seamen, gunners, marines,
> The crews of the gig and the yawl,
> The bearded man and the lad in his teens,
> Carpenters, coal passers – all.
> Then, knocking the ashes from out of his pipe,
> Said Burke in an offhand way:
> 'We're all in that dead man's list, by Cripe!
> Kelly and Burke and Shea.'
> 'Oh, the fighting races don't die out,
> If they seldom die in bed,
> For love is first in their hearts, no doubt.'
> Said Burke: then Kelly said:
> 'When Michael, the Irish Archangel, stands,
> The angel with the sword,
> And the battle-dead from a hundred lands
> Are ranged in one big horde,
> Our line, that for Gabriel's trumpet waits,
> Will stretch three deep that day,
> From Jehoshaphat to the Golden Gates –
> Kelly and Burke and Shea.'
> 'Well, here's thank God for the race and the sod!'
> Said Kelly and Burke and Shea'.

6

I Shall be a Slave to Nothing

It was during Michael's 'blast and bloody' days as a young man in London that he first took up smoking and drinking with the boys. It was also around this time that Moya Llewelyn Davies, who along with her husband Crompton, first met Michael through his sister Hannie, the pair becoming part of Moya's Irish circle of friends living in London. Moya's first impression of Michael however was not very flattering. All she could remember was his 'endless smoking and big talk!'

He usually smoked 'Three Castles' a well-known brand of English cigarettes at that time and got through between forty to fifty a day. Around 1919 he decided cigarettes were taking over his life and gave up completely, saying to his sister Katie: 'I shall be a slave to nothing!' Although even before then, he occasionally gave up smoking for a few days or even weeks, just to prove that he could be strong willed when he wanted to. However he continued to carry cigarettes, usually in a silver case, to offer others, especially to soldiers, detectives and Auxiliaries during the War of Independence, but was rarely again to smoke himself, an example of amazing willpower, especially considering the stress he was under during that time.

Unlike smoking, Michael was never a heavy drinker except possibly during those 'blast and bloody' days as a youth in London, of which little is known. It was around that period he got in with a hard-drinking, hard-living crowd of Irishmen and although he never lost his faith, he also went through a very anti-Catholic, anti-religious phase. His use of swearing, cursing and telling bawdy jokes, also occurred around this period, and was to stay with him for the rest of his life.

Michael was never a great lover of porter, although he seemed to have enjoyed a glass of the local West Cork 'Clonakilty Wrastler' whenever he was down in that area visiting his family and friends. He did, however, enjoy the occasional sweet sherry or port and when he was in a state of exhaustion from overwork, lack of food, or both, the odd drop of Jameson's whiskey or a brandy usually revived him. One drink he was particularly fond of was brandy, with a dash of curacao.

As the War of Independence became more intense, Michael, for security reasons often chose hotels or public houses to meet his colleagues, spies, messengers, etc. He would usually refer to them as 'joints'. The list was numerous, Clearys, Devlins, The Stag's Head and many others, with Vaughan's Hotel in Rutland Square (now Parnell Square) being 'joint' number one. Such locations did not arise the suspicion of the RIC, 'G' men, military or other potential enemies. When new Volunteers came up to Dublin to meet Michael for the first time, after the business was done, he would take them to a nearby bar and buy a round of drinks. This would help them to relax and then their true personality would come to the fore. Michael being a good psychologist would soon learn if they were up to the tasks he had set them.

As the War of Independence became more intense, Michael, whilst on a job, always made a rule of 'no booze'. This was not only applicable to himself but also his men. He knew the effect that alcohol could have on the mind, as well as the body, and that both he and the boys had to be alert and ready for action at a moment's notice. Obviously, when meeting associates in pubs or hotels, he too would have to order a drink so as not to arouse suspicion. This was usually a small sherry or port, of which he rarely took more than a couple of sips.

During the time of the Treaty, whilst Michael was in London as one of the five plenipotentiaries, there were rumours of heavy drinking by the delegation. He and Griffith were even accused of being drunk, drugged, or both, by their enemies when they signed the Treaty on 6 December 1921. Nothing could have been further from the truth. Apart from anything else, Michael was suffering badly from a stomach ulcer, and heavy drinking was the last thing he would have indulged in.

The view from Michael's cell in Sligo Jail – in April 1918 he spent about three weeks in solitary confinement [see p. 68]

7

MICHAEL, THE MAN WHO LOVED HIS FOOD AND ALSO LOVED A JOKE

Michael love of food and equally his love of horseplay were legendary along with his genius for repartee and witty one-liners. Occasionally he combined the two.

There were many times, especially during the 1919–21 period, when Michael was lucky to grab a sandwich and a mug of tea, during those frantic twenty-hour days. He loved his breakfast – rashers, eggs, sausages or black pudding, with fresh soda bread, all washed down with mugs of hot, strong tea into which he heaped two large spoonfuls of sugar. In Michael's time, as now, a good Irish breakfast would set anyone up for the day, as well as being a filling meal at any time.

There is an interesting story associated with Ireland's traditional breakfast and Michael's family. It was his maternal grandmother Johanna O'Brien, who had the original recipe for the now famous Clonakilty Black Pudding. There was a long tradition in country areas – having killed a pig to make black pudding for the family – to sell any surplus to the local butcher. The O'Brien's black pudding was very popular with the people of Clonakilty and when Johanna was old, she decided to sell her precious recipe to a local butcher, Philip Harrington. When the Harrington's sold their business to a Patrick McSweeny in 1968, they also passed on the O'Brien recipe. A nephew of Patrick's, Edward Twomey, decided to start producing the black pudding commercially and it can now be bought in shops and supermarkets all over Ireland, as well as in delicatessens both in the United Kingdom and across Europe.

Even as a young boy, Michael was full of mischief and practical jokes. He spent a lot of time with one of his cousins Jim Collins, who was about two years older than him. Although Michael had been baptised at Rosscarbery, he and his family went to mass at the new church at Lisavaird as it was only a couple of miles away from Woodfield. Both Michael and Jim became altar boys at the newly built church, but never took their roles very seriously., giggling and pulling faces during services. They were forever playing pranks and making mistakes, which both thought hilarious. However, many years later, during the height of the War of Independence, a far more serious and devout Michael was again to assist at Sunday Mass, this time at the Pro Cathedral in Dublin. Although many of his friends and colleagues criticised him for taking such an unnecessary risk, his reply was he felt safest in God's house and amongst a large crowd.

Around 1900 when the new house was being built at Woodfield, Jim and Michael helped with the building, by visiting a nearby quarry with an old wheelbarrow to collect stones. One of Michael's favourite tricks was to persuade his cousin Jim to sit in the wheelbarrow for a ride. Then he would rush to the quarry's edge and let go of the handles. Fortunately, the barrow always scraped to a stop just in time. A traumatic experience for the hapless passenger!

Joe O'Reilly, Michael's ever-faithful servant, friend and general dogs-body, had known him since their early days in London. Unfortunately he was also to be the main butt of Michael's unmerciful teasing, baiting and sometimes cruel humour. An early example of this took place on Christmas Eve 1916, when Michael and Gearóid O'Sullivan, having finally been released from Frongoch Camp in North Wales, decided to call in and see their old friend in Dublin, before heading down to West Cork for the Christmas. Joe had left Frongoch a few weeks earlier and returned to the city, sharing a room with another friend. Early that morning the pair burst into Joe's room and an exuberant and somewhat inebriated Michael (he had been carousing all night on the steamer from Holyhead) inflicted one of his famous 'Collins' kisses' (both ears bitten and bleeding!) and bear hugs on the poor, half asleep Joe. He then pulled out an almost full bottle of port from his overcoat pocket and proceeded to pour the contents down Joe's throat. The pair then left a rather battered and somewhat inebriated Joe, to explain to his baffled room mate that it was only the Big Fellow's idea of fun.

The abiding memory people have who knew and worked with Michael was his love of practical jokes, schoolboy banter, witty one-liners and occasionally merciless teasing. However, it was for his love of a 'bit of ear' that he was best remembered. This rough and tumble wrestling match, which first manifested itself when he was a schoolboy, involved grappling ones opponent and pulling them down onto the ground, and then biting the ear of the unfortunate victim, until they begged for mercy. Sometimes they were lucky enough to receive a 'Collins' kiss'. It was however, during those traumatic years from 1917 up to the Truce in July 1921, when each day could be their last, or worse, facing imprisonment and torture that Michael and his companions found it was a way of letting off steam. The wrestling bouts and no holds-bared scrimmages with Harry Boland, his cousin Gearóid O'Sullivan or Liam Tobin, was the horseplay of desperate men engaged in a deadly war.

Up to the last day of his life, Michael enjoyed his 'bit of ear'. On 21 August 1922 Michael and Emmet Dalton, were staying at the Imperial Hotel in Cork city, as the nearby army barracks had recently been burnt by the anti-Treatyites. They had just returned from a tour around West Cork, when an old friend of Michael's called in to urge him to find a solution to the Civil War that was wrecking havoc on the new state. They argued together and Michael told him to come back the next day as he hoped he would have some better news for him. Then Michael, Commander-in-Chief of the new Free State army challenged his old friend to a 'bit of ear' and the pair ended up rolling around on the floor of the hotel, much to the alarm and perplexity of the sentries.

However, they had already learned what it was to be like on the receiving end of Michael's boisterous moods. Only the previous evening he had returned to the

Tom Cullen, Michael Collins and Liam Tobin

hotel, to meet his sister Mary Collins-Powell and his nephew Seán, for tea, when he found the two soldiers, supposedly on sentry duty in the hotel's foyer, leaning up against each other, half asleep. Michael strode up to them, banged their heads together, and then marched on into the dining-room to meet his sister and her son, without saying a word.

Seán Collins-Powell summed up the incident, during a RTE television interview in the late 1980s, 'It was his gesture to say he knew what went on, he just bumped their heads together, cut out the nonsense and got on with the business'.

The people whose homes he used as 'safe-houses' were often on the receiving end of Michael's boisterous high jinks. When he and Gearóid O'Sullivan first stayed with the O'Donovan family in Rathgar, they were given the front bedroom in the house. However, after a couple of nights, the pair were transferred to a back bedroom, because of their noisy wrestling matches and Michael's annoying habit of pulling hairs out of Gearóid's leg, to wake him up in the morning. This caused the victim to awake with a scream and could easily have drawn unwanted attention to the house from passers by.

Michael was always an early riser and would make sure that the rest of his sleeping companions were as well. Jugs of cold water, fire hoses, pulling off the bedclothes and even lifting up the beds and tipping his somewhat dazed colleagues out on to the cold floor were all the normal alarm calls from Mr. Collins!

Occasionally this maniacal, high-spirited Michael could wreck a room in a pub or hotel. Devlins, now demolished, a pub opposite the Rotunda Hospital in Parnell Street, often providing accommodation for him and his friends, was an example. An old colleague of Michael's remembered thus, although I think his account is somewhat over dramatised: 'When Mr Devlin met Collins he handed over a neatly furnished room. Within the month, it was a wreck. There was scarcely a chair with a back to it, the Delft (earthenware pottery) had disappeared. Yet when one of the gang, hearing a rumble of thunder from the sitting-room in which Collins was lashing out with a chair, apologised to the Devlins, they merely smiled and said, "It eases his mind!" They spoke with an understanding of love, for it was in this savage lashing and straining that all the accumulated anxiety was released.'

During the height of the Black and Tan war around 1920, Michael was up to his usual buffoonery despite the seriousness of the situation. He, along with his companions, had attended an evening meeting at a house in Palmerston Park, Rathgar, to discuss the IRB's role in shaping events in the ongoing struggle with the British. After a heated four-hour meeting, most of the participants were tired and as they were staying the night at the house, went up to bed. Michael however was not in the mood for sleep and instead, as Liam Deasy one of Cork's leading IRA men later recalled, visited every bedroom and started a pillow fight. By four o'clock, when he himself finally fell asleep from sheer exhaustion, there was nothing to be seen in any of the bedrooms but feathers from ceiling to floor!

When friends and colleagues visited Michael at another of his safe-houses, this time situated in Drumcondra, word soon got around to decline Michael's offer of a boat trip along the Tolka River which ran behind the safe-house in Richmond Road. A small rowing boat was moored at the end of the garden and was intended for emergency getaways. Across the river at that time were still green fields and open country, bordering onto the grounds of Croke Park, home of newly founded Gaelic Athletic Association. Michael would enjoy taking his friends out for boat trips but sometimes, if he was in one of his mischievous moods, his unfortunate passengers could find themselves in the river instead of on it, having been pushed overboard by their boatman!

During the War of Independence, Michael often met his double agents, Broy, Kavanagh and Dave Neligan at Tommy Gay's house in Haddon Road, Clontarf. Gay, a librarian, worked as one of Michael's undercover intelligence men, and lived in what was then, and still is, a quiet, pleasant residential area along Dublin Bay's north-side. The men would all travel separately to the house, either by tram or bicycle so as not to arouse any suspicion. After their meetings, Mrs Gay would give them tea, accompanied with her delicious homemade pancakes, which Michael would always scoff down with great delight.

An amusing story was told by Michael's close friend Batt O'Connor, who along with his wife and children, frequently let Michael use their home in Brendan Road, Donnybrook as one of his many safe-houses. The use of houses with young children was always a good cover for Michael, and rarely aroused suspicion of the RIC or British army, as it gave him the appearance of a visiting uncle or brother.

Around the time of the Truce, July–August 1921 when Batt, along with Michael and another friend Con Collins (no relation), had been to a colleague's house for a drink and to discuss the latest political situation in Ireland. Upon their rather late return to the O'Connor's residence, Mrs O'Connor seeing her guests were in need of some refreshments, hastily prepared a quick supper of sausages and fried eggs. That evening, Michael, in one of his mischievous moods, began to taunt Con, poking fun at him, half in jest, half in earnest. As Michael continued his banter, Con, rather embarrassed, kept glancing away. Each time his eyes left the plate, Michael would dart his fork into Con's sausages, until the Big Fellow had consumed all but one. Finally, Con looking down at his now depleted plate, confessed he really could not remember eating the sausages so quickly. Michael quietly chuckled to himself, saying nothing.

Eileen, Batt's daughter, remembered many years later how much Michael enjoyed her mother's cooking. Mrs O'Connor always delighted in preparing wholesome and attractive meals for him and his friends. He was particularly fond of one of her specialities, marmalade pudding, with marmalade sauce. In fact, Michael was quite fond of oranges, and when feeling poorly would get Joe O'Reilly to make him up a hot orange drink, possibly with a dash of Jameson's whiskey.

Card-playing was another pursuit in which Michael was inclined to show the same manic intensity that he brought to bear on most things he did. It was as a prisoner in Frongoch that he first became interested in card games, one of the few diversions that helped while away the time in the camp. Later, during the War of Independence, as he travelled around Ireland conferring with local commandants, inspecting camps and expanding his intelligence network, he often went by train, and to break the monotony of the journey would play a game of cards, usually whist, with his companions. This was also the case on his frequent trips to London during and after the Treaty in 1921–22, with the journey from Dublin, via Holyhead, taking up to ten hours on a good run and even longer in adverse weather. However, as long as Michael had a good hand, all was well, but if dealt a poor one, he rapidly lost interest in the game. He would then look into his fellow-players cards, upset the deck or create a diversion by slapping a colleague on the back so hard that they dropped their cards or even drag the likely winner on to the floor for a 'bit of ear'. As with everything in his life, *Michael had to win.*

Michael's schoolboy pranks were innate and part of his character. However, it was his male colleagues who were at the receiving end, the women in his life usually escaped his buffoonery and were normally treated with great respect and courtesy. An interesting insight into Michael's behaviour from a woman's point of view was to be found in a letter from Moya Llewelyn Davies to Piaras Béaslaí written some fifteen years after his death in October 1937: 'Personally I found Mick's practical-joke habits rather tiresome, although I didn't come in contact with them, a boring form of amusement only suitable for schoolboys.' She did, however, come into contact with his occasional 'bear' hugs!

Michael's 'bear hugs' given to both men and women were another idiosyncrasy. Being a very strong and muscular man, Michael did not always realise his own strength and his natural exuberance on greeting someone and giving them a friendly hug, could sometimes be quite a painful experience to the recipient! In fact, his 'bear hug' to Seán MacEoin nearly re-hospitalised the poor man. Seán the legendary 'Blacksmith of Ballinalee' had earlier that year, 1921, been involved in an armed raid against the British. Unfortunately, he had been caught, shot through the lung and savagely beaten by the Black and Tans before being imprisoned in Mountjoy Jail. He was then convicted of murder and sentenced to be hung. Michael made various attempts to rescue him but to no avail. However, when the Truce was announced in July of that year, Michael insisted that no talks could go ahead until MacEoin was released.

A few days after leaving Mountjoy, MacEoin paid a visit to Vaughan's Hotel in Rutland Square, now Parnell Square, to meet Michael and to thank him for all he had done in getting him out of prison. As he walked into the lobby, Michael spying him from the landing above, vaulted the banisters in a flying leap, crashed down on his still ailing friend, giving him one of his famous 'bear hugs' – Mac-Eoin's recovery was to take a few days longer!

During the Treaty discussions in London, in late 1921, the main Irish delegation, along with their secretaries and staff, who were based at 10 Hans Place, decided to have a party and invited Michael and his colleagues along. The rest of the delegation, including Michael, were staying at 15 Cadogan Gardens, a few minutes walk away from Hans Place. Shortly after their arrival, Michael and his colleagues, who preferred horseplay to formalities, began throwing cushions, tangerine oranges, apples and nuts from the table, and even coal from the coal-scuttles. Michael was, as usual, the main instigator of such mayhem.

Another example of Michael's love of banter, and food, was recalled by the vice-president of the Provisional Government, W. T. Cosgrave, in early 1922. He remembered Michael's frequent visits, accompanied by Oliver St John Gogarty, to the Cosgrave home in Templeogue, at the foothills of the Dublin Mountains, during the first six months of that year. Although Michael had known Gogarty throughout the War of Independence, sometimes using his home as a safe house, it was not until around 1922 that the two men became close friends. Michael, having a highly developed sense of humour, took great delight in Gogarty's company, roaring with laughter at his often irreverent sallies. Cosgrave was to recall 'That the two rascals took more delight in shocking me than in talking serious business when they came out for tea.' He also remembered that both Gogarty and Michael would always consume large quantities of cake and sweet tea during their visits.

Michael Collins and Arthur Griffiths at Seán MacEoin's wedding, June 1922

Left: *22 Hans Place, London* and right: *15 Cadogan Gardens, London used by Michael and the Irish delegation during the Treaty negotiations*

Another incident, again in 1922, that illustrates Michael's enjoyment of sweet food was at a party held at Furry Park House, Killester by Moya Llewelyn Davies. This well documented occasion involved an attempted assassination on Michael just a few days before he was killed in August. Surrounded by many well-known people including George Bernard Shaw, Christabel Pankhurst, the Laverys, Piaras Béaslaí, to name just a few, Michael was sitting in the large bay window of Moya's drawing-room. Word was received that an attempt was to be made on his life that evening. However, he refused to move away from the window and continued eating the cream buns. It was left to faithful Joe O'Reilly and Hazel Lavery to stand behind him, shielding him from danger for the duration of the party. Later that night a sniper was eventually found in the grounds of the house and taken down to the slob lands by Michael's men and shot dead.

Michael is also remembered for his genius with repartee, along with his witty but often caustic one-liners. He was, from a youth, a great admirer of Oscar Wilde, a fellow Irishman and perhaps the greatest master of unconventional wit and love of paradox.

At a meeting in Southwark, London in 1915, held to encourage young Irishmen to join Captain John Redmond in Flanders, the speaker described Redmond as 'a man I would go to hell and back with'. From the back of the hall came Michael's unmistakable West Cork accent: 'I'd not trouble about the return portion of the ticket!'

During the Rising in the GPO, one the first things Michael did was to empty the contents of the beer kegs he found stored in the building saying 'They said we were drunk in '98. They won't be able to say that now.' Later, also in the GPO as the shelling and general mayhem reached its height, Michael was to comment, 'I was the only man in the whole place who wasn't at confession or communion.'

Michael's sense of humour prevailed even during the height of the fighting in the GPO when he, along with Gearóid O'Sullivan went up to the somewhat harassed and exhausted Pádraig Pearse and asked 'Would he mind if they popped out for a bit, as they had arranged a date with a couple of girls and didn't want to stand them up?' Pearse's reply was unprintable!

Later, summing up the Rising, Michael said, 'It was the greatest bloody fiasco that we ever engaged in. There was courage, there was patriotism but there was bloody all else. There was no organisation! We were like lambs to the slaughter. 'Noble' they called it. 'Shameful' I'd call it."

During the War of Independence, Michael summed up his actions on Bloody Sunday: 'I found out those fellows we put on the spot were going to put a lot of us on the spot, so I got there first!' Later that day he reflected sadly, 'When will it all end? When can a man get down to a book and peace?'

Just before the Treaty talks, Winston Churchill commented rhetorically: 'Where was Michael Collins during the Great War? To us he would have been worth a dozen brass hats'. Later, when Churchill finally met Michael he said: 'Well sir, you are a more important man now than I was in the Boer War. I only had £100 on my head, you had £10,000.'

'Ah yes sir, but you are not allowing for inflation, I fear!' Michael replied.

In 1921, as the Treaty talks got under way with Lloyd George and his cabinet in London, Michael discovered that on his way to mass one morning he was being followed. Later that day he said to Lloyd George: 'I hope your man was a Catholic, as I don't wish to be accused of conversion, as well as subversion!' Around the same time he wrote to a fellow Irishman and personal friend in London, John O'Kane, about the lack of trust between the Irish plenipotentiaries: 'To go for a drink is one thing, to be driven to it is another.' Earlier during the Treaty talks, he had written to O'Kane, summing up the English delegation. 'Theirs is a nest of singing birds. They chirrup mightily one to the other – and there's the falseness of it all, because no one trusts the other.'

8

MICHAEL, JEKYLL AND HYDE

It was possible Michael suffered from a slight form of manic depression, which manifested itself in his dramatic mood swings, alternating from elation to depression, and back to his normal high spirits, often within a very short space of time. Many outstanding charismatic leaders were also fellow sufferers – Julius Caesar, Winston Churchill and Napoleon. However, with the latter, at least Michael was in good company – Napoleon was his hero and in some ways his role model.

Michael was a very complex person – highlighted, in particular by the two sides of his personality, the bullying, domineering man as against the gentle, considerate, good-hearted one. He could be either extremely kind or very ruthless. If someone had to be killed or a job done, Michael had no second thoughts, the deed had to be carried out. It was paradoxical that here was a man whose feelings could so easily get hurt by another person's reaction towards him, after he had himself been rude or bombastic to them.

He was certainly a very demanding taskmaster and a perfectionist. Michael set himself high standards and expected those around him to do the same. He did not suffer fools and had no hesitation in letting people know this.

Joe O'Reilly, being the closest to him throughout the War of Independence and afterwards, was to bear the brunt of not only Michael's schoolboy pranks, but also his frequent rages. He would 'let off steam' to Joe when things went wrong or people did not come up to his high expectations. Joe had the unenviable task of trying to soothe and calm Michael.

As far back as their London days together before 1916, Joe was at the receiving end of his bullying tactics. A typical example was when they both attended a GAA sports day held at Herne Hill and were running in a race together. Towards the finish, both were neck and neck. Michael, determined to win by whatever means, put on a spurt and as he flew past Joe, deliberately dug his elbow into the soft part of Joe's arm. He won the race, but the watching crowd and his fellow competitors saw his tactics. After the race Michael and Joe spent the next ten minutes arguing as to who had won, although the result was patently obvious, to competitors and onlookers alike.

This negative streak was also to appear when Michael played hurling with his local team in London, the Geraldines. He was known to fly into a temper if he suspected foul play and tended to dominate the team with his intimidating manner. Even during that period, he was to make a few enemies amongst his fellow players because of his bullying tactics. The game had to be played by his rules, and his rules alone!

Michael's could occasionally be quite scathing and sarcastic. If someone upset him, he was inclined to reply with a few oaths thrown in for good measure! However, he was at heart very sensitive and when his abrupt and surly behaviour backfired, he would make every endeavour to make amends to the offended party.

Occasionally, Michael could be very arrogant, insolent, stiff-necked and rude. If he was in a hurry, he had no time for social niceties, often failing to shake hands or wish people good day. This attitude occasionally upset some women, who were repelled by his brusqueness and lack of common courtesy, in an age when men usually treated the fairer sex with great politeness and consideration.

Michael knew he could be a difficult person to get along with, and that he was often unreasonable and frequently his temper had an exceedingly short fuse. Unfortunately because of his abrupt and volatile nature, Michael easily offended people and, unwittingly in later life, made many enemies, some of whom had previously been good friends. Michael's relationship with Austin Stack is an example of this.

A fellow member of the Supreme Council of the IRB, as well as Minister for Home Affairs in the first Dáil, Stack had been a close friend since 1917. They corresponded frequently and Michael personally helped 'spring' Stack from Manchester prison in 1919. However, Stack was not very competent in running his department and around 1920, during a cabinet meeting, in front of their fellow ministers, Michael accused Stack's department as 'Being a bloody joke!' On another occasion, Michael referred back to 1916, when Stack had been commandant of the local Kerry Brigade. Stack's party had failed to rescue Sir Roger Casement, after he stepped ashore from a German submarine at Banna Strand. Michael frequently referred to this incident and Stack's incompetence at the time. Sadly, the friendship between the two men was to end and Stack transferred his allegiance from Michael to Cathal Brugha, a man who never had much time for Michael Collins because of his IRB activities. Brugha had always strongly disapproved of the IRB – in fact he disliked any secret organisations.

Another example of Michael's volatile nature in upsetting people that were close to him occurred between himself and his second cousin Nancy O'Brien. Perhaps being related, they understood each other and Nancy being the sort of woman she was, strong minded and strong willed, would give as good as she got from her cousin Michael, which he enjoyed and liked in a woman. Nancy and Michael knew one another for many years. They had both gone to England and worked for the Post Office Savings Bank in London and returned to Ireland before the Rising in 1916. Nancy continued working for the civil service, this time at the GPO in Dublin. Around 1919, Sir James McMahon, head of the department of post and telegrams, selected her to be his confidential clerk, to decode the top secret messages between Whitehall and Dublin Castle. Curiously, the British never realised her relationship with Michael, and upon her new appointment she immediately contacted her cousin to offer what help she could to him.

Her lunch times would be spent, usually in the ladies toilet in the GPO, making copies of decoded messages and then hiding them, in either her hair or on her person. Later, she would arrange to meet Michael, or one of his men, usually at her lodgings in Glasnevin, a residential area about two miles north of Dublin city centre. All went well until one day Michael gave her a severe grilling about an urgent message he was expecting. Nancy had no knowledge of the message and explained to him that the only thing she had received was a rather silly love letter from an unknown admirer. Michael exploded in his usual way and called her amongst other names an 'Gligeen ejit!' Nancy turned on him angrily, saying that having put her life on the line for him over the last six months, all she ever got in return was abuse and contempt. She told him where he could stuff his messages and that he could run his own 'bloody war' in future! Nancy then stormed off, leaving him dumbstruck.

A few hours later around 2 a.m., Nancy was to hear the sound of gravel being flung against her bedroom window. On looking out, she saw Michael standing in the garden below, beckoning her down. She realised that he had risked his life cycling across the city during the curfew to see her, and quickly flung on her dressing-gown and went down to meet him. There at the front door he apologised profusely, full of remorse for his short temper, explaining it was partly due the great strain he was under at the time. Then as he was leaving, he said, 'I've left a little present for you' – a bag of 'bull's eyes', one of her favourite sweets. After that incident, Michael always treated his cousin with great respect, and never again, in her company, let his temper get the better of him.

Throughout his short but amazing life, Michael always wanted to be 'top dog' and to run the show, whether it was in sport, work or eventually the fight to gain Ireland's freedom. In his various offices scattered around Dublin, he had a habit of marking certain files 'DBI' meaning 'Don't Butt In!' If anyone did 'butt in' then they ran the full gauntlet of Michael's fury. However, he himself frequently stuck his nose into everyone else's affairs and did not hesitate to tell them how they should run things.

It is possible that this streak in Michael's nature was one of the things that upset De Valera on his return from America after eighteen months of fund-raising for the new Republic. As De Valera disembarked from the ship at Custom House Quay, in the early hours of 23 December 1920, he was greeted by two of Michael's old friends, Batt O'Connor and Tom Cullen. De Valera asked the men how things were going since he had been away and Tom replied, 'Great! The Big Fellow is leading us and everything is going marvellous.'

De Valera, slapping the guard-rail with his hand, snarled 'Big Fellow, we'll see who's the Big Fellow!'

The other side to Michael's personality was his charm, kindness and thoughtfulness for those around him, traits inherited in part from his mother. He had a great compassion and love for children, the old and the downtrodden. His vibrant and ebullient nature was infectious. His disarming 'little boy' smile would mollify most people who met him, often within seconds of being on the receiving end of one of his explosive tempers. He possessed a natural charm and bonhomie and exuded an aura of confidence that inspired both men and women who worked or helped him. His presence made them feel safe, strong and fearless, and enabled them to undertake the most dangerous of missions. He could win them over with just a slap on the back, a laugh or a smile. But more often just one look from those deep-set, grey penetrating eyes, would not only disarm his critics but have most people totally under his spell. They would happily go ahead risking life and limb to undertake whatever mission he set them, remembering only the better side of his nature.

There are many stories of his kindness and generosity, but the one thing that always stands out is his amazing capacity to remember each person as an individual, their names, what they were fond of and how to make them happy – a landlady's particular brand of sherry, or a plug of tobacco for an old colleague down on his luck, etc. Sometimes, it could be a small bottle of whiskey or cigarettes for a friend in hospital or prison, he even remembered the type of tea or sweetmeats (chocolates or sugar coated preserved fruits) a person enjoyed.

An example of this happened to his friend and ally Moya Llewelyn Davies who was not only very partial to sweetmeats, but also 'China' tea, which was and still is, difficult to find in Dublin. She, along with two other women, Eileen Mac-Grane and Patricia Hoey, were arrested after a raid by the Black and Tans in March 1921, who had been tipped off about suspicious goings-on at Moya's house, Furry Park, Killester in North Dublin. Moya and her two companions were taken to Mount-joy Jail and held there for a few months until the Truce, although no charge was brought against any of them. During their internment, Michael managed to smuggle woollen rugs, books, China tea and Moya's favourite sweetmeats, into the prison, right under the noses of the guards.

Dan Breen was another recipient of Michael's thoughtfulness. Dan, a native of Grange in Co. Tipperary, had joined the IRB and later the local flying column under Seán Treacy, another Tipperary man. He was one of the main participants of the Solo-headbeg ambush , which initiated the start of the War of Independence on 21 January 1919. Some months later, Dan was in Dublin working for Michael and during a raid by British soldiers on a friend's house in Drumcondra, was nearly caught. Whilst trying to escape out of a bedroom window, Dan instead of landing in the garden, unfortunately fell through the roof of a recently constructed conservatory and was badly cut. Despite his injuries, he managed to escape and found refuge at another friend's house, where arrangements were made for him to be smuggled into the nearby Mater Hospital to received proper medical attention. Shortly after he arrived a young nurse came to take his temperature and check his dressings. As she was leaving, she whispered to Dan, 'You might appreciate your medicine under the pillow!' It was a plug of his favourite tobacco, Mick McQuaid, along with a small bottle of Jameson's whiskey – a present from the Big Fellow!

There were many instances when Michael, feeling very guilty, dispatched Joe O'Reilly around Dublin purchasing flowers, chocolates, sometimes even champagne, to make amends to those he upset. There was even an occasion, around 1919, when he wrote to his sister Hannie, who was still living in England, to call into all the local tobacconists in West London, and find a particular brand of tobacco for Austin Stack, who was in prison at the time.

The O'Connor family always remembered his kindness and loyalty. Michael was very close to the family and particularly Batt, who he first met at Larkfield in early 1916. This was the home of the Nationalist and Republican Count Plunkett in Kimmage, a suburb of south-west Dublin near the Dublin Mountains. In an adjoining field to the house, a training camp had been set up for the Volunteers, many from England including Michael, who had returned to their native land. After the Easter Rising, both men were interned at Frongoch, where their friendship grew. Later, during the War of Independence, Michael frequently used Batt's home in Brendan Road as a safe-house. The children were particularly fond of their 'Uncle Mick', who always found time to play with them and listen to their prayers. When Batt was in hospital after a serious car accident, Michael, despite his heavy workload, called around most evenings to see Mrs O'Connor and the children, to check how they were or if they needed anything.

Another well-known example of Michael's kindness and thoughtfulness was to the De Valera family. When De Valera was away fund-raising in America for eighteen months, Michael, during the height of the War of Independence, and with a curfew in place all around Dublin, risked his life once a week, to travel down to Greystones and give urgently needed Green Cross money to Sinead, Dev's wife, and to play with De Valera's children. They too fondly remembered their 'Uncle Mick'.

On the last day of his life, Michael was to be remembered for his thoughtfulness. Early in the morning of Tuesday 22 August, as he was coming out of the Victoria Hotel in Macroom, an old lady came up to Michael and asked 'Are you still in charge around here?'

'Yes I am', Michael replied.

'Well,' said the old lady, 'during the War of Independence your lads blew up the bridge just down from my cottage, so now I'm unable to take my donkey and cart to the local creamery unless I take the long way round'.

Michael promised her he would see what he could do about getting the bridge repaired. That evening Michael was killed but his instructions were carried out and two days later a party of Free State soldiers came and repaired the bridge.

Michael's kindness also came out in his numerous correspondence. Often, after his secretary had typed up a letter, before he would add his own personal note, inquiring after the recipient's health or family, or adding some personal comment. People meant a lot to him and he would treat each as an individual. He was not ashamed to cry or laugh with them, and any misfortunes that befell them would upset him too, especially if in some way he was responsible. He was a man of great confidence, and inspired trust in the majority who met him. Michael, despite his temper and impatient manner, was at heart more Hyde than Jekyll. He was, and still is, referred to as 'The Laughing Boy' – the Michael most people remember.

Michael's pistol – worn when he became Commander-in-Chief of the Free State army
[Cathal Brugha Barracks]

9

ROMANCE AND THE WOMEN IN MICHAEL'S LIFE

Women played a crucial role in both Michael's personal and working life. Being born into a predominately female household, his mother, grandmother and five sisters all influenced him as a young boy. They were strong, dominant and resourceful women and as he grew into manhood he was to have a natural respect for women of a similar calibre, many of whom were to work with him later during the War of Independence. He was usually more at ease in the company of slightly older women, two examples being Hazel Lavery and Moya Llewelyn Davies, both of whom were around ten years his senior. Although as a teenager he often felt awkward in female company, as many young men do as they mature to adulthood, Michael soon developed into what is known as a 'ladies' man. His natural good looks, personality, charm and innate use of flattery, was always to stand him in good stead with the many women he was to meet during his life.

Michael was a normal heterosexual young man but was also, for most of his life, a devout Catholic. He came from a strong moral family background and upbringing and this morality was to continue up until his death. Michael, along with his friends and companions, had high principles and a great respect for women generally.

Despite this, there were, and still are, rumours linked with him having affairs with, Moya and Hazel, both of whom were not only older than Michael, but also married and upper-class. As already mentioned, Michael first encountered both women whilst living in London, Moya around 1910 and Hazel in 1913, through his sister Hannie. After Michael returned to Ireland in early 1916, he did not meet Hazel again until the autumn of 1921, during the Treaty talks in London. Moya, however, moved back to Ireland around 1919 and became one of his most loyal and helpful friends, as well as being a secret member of Cumann na mBan, the women's branch of the Irish Volunteers.

I use the word secret because once a woman started to work for Michael, either as a secretary or in any other capacity, he forbade them to be involved openly in the Cumann na mBan movement. He did not want them drawing attention to themselves by going to parades or meetings, but more especially, he did not want them wearing their Cumann na mBan uniforms in public. Michael hated women wearing uniforms of any kind and perhaps this was a factor in his indifferent relationship with Countess Markievicz. She liked uniforms and first appeared fully dressed in her Citizen Army outfit, breeches and all, during the 1916 Rising and later at Thomas Ashe's funeral in 1917.

After his mother died in April 1907 from stomach cancer, at a relatively young age of 52, Michael's sister Hannie, who he was living with in London, was to take over the 'motherly' role and try to steer the young Michael along the 'straight and narrow' pathway of life. It is interesting to note that both Hannie and Michael must have journeyed back to Woodfield in West Cork from London, to attend their mother's funeral. Whether they had travelled home to see her upon hearing that her death from cancer was imminent, or returned after she had died, is unknown, although most likely the former is the case, considering the time it would have taken to travel from London to West Cork. Their attendance as chief mourners at their mother's funeral, held two days after her death, along with their brother Johnny, sisters and numerous relations and friends was noted in the local *West Cork People* newspaper. The paper's editor at the time was Michael's brother-in-law, Patrick O'Driscoll.

Romance was first to enter into Michael's life around 1910, when he became friendly with some of the Irish girls who worked with him at the Post Office Savings Bank in Hammersmith, London. Nancy O'Brien, his second cousin, was to comment that 'all the girls were mad about him', and he soon realised that his athletic build, good looks and boyish charm, would win the hearts of many a colleen. It was around this period he first became friendly with Dolly Brennan a Dublin girl, who was also Nancy O'Brien's best friend. However, it was not until 1914 that his first real romance with a young, bright intelligent girl from Moloskey, near Mullagh, Co. Clare, Susan Killeen, blossomed.

The pair not only shared similar interests in poetry and books but also in Irish history and politics. They both belonged to the Gaelic League and frequently attended ceilidhes and meetings together at various venues in north and west London. Susan at that time shared lodgings with Nancy O'Brien, Michael's second cousin, as well as working with her at the Post Office Savings Bank in Hammersmith. Michael wrote his romantic Valentine's day 1916 poem to Susan (see Chapter 5), as well as numerous letters and poems when he was later interned in Frongoch. Around 1915, Susan lost her job at the post office, as she refused to take the oath of allegiance to the British crown and returned to Dublin to work in P. S. O'Hegarty's bookshop in Dawson Street. Later, during the War of Independence, this location was used as one of Michael's main dispatch centres. It was also around this time, 1915, that she and Nancy lodged with Mrs Quick in Howth, a small fishing village about ten miles north of Dublin city centre. Michael and Seán Hurley along with Joe O'Reilly used to meet the girls in Howth, for a couple of days, on their way home from England for holidays in West Cork. Michael developed a real affection for Howth, and returned as often as he could in the years ahead. I have been told there is a photograph taken of Susan and Michael together on Howth pier, with the lighthouse and Ireland's Eye in the background, but was unable to find it.

However, by 1917, Michael's romantic relationship with Susan Killeen turned platonic although they remained friends and allies until early 1922. Susan disagreed with him over the Treaty and was not happy about his new romance with Kitty Kiernan. Michael may have proposed to her sometime during their relationship, as later on Susan accused him of just wanting a wife who would run around after him, cook his meals, wash his clothes and bear his children! Around 1920 Susan returned to Co. Clare, this time to Ennis, working for one of the new Land Banks set up in 1919 by Michael in connection with the Dáil Loan and it was here she met her future husband Denis O'Dea. They married in 1923 and resided in Granard, Co. Longford, the hometown of Kitty Kiernan. The Land Bank later became known as the Bank of Ireland and Denis was for a while manager of the Granard branch. Denis died in 1953 and his wife Susan died some years later in 1970.

Around 1917, the new woman in Michael's life was Madeline (Dilly) Dicker who was about nine years younger than him. She was very attractive, vivacious and full of fun, as well as being musical – she used to play the piano at the local cinema to accompany the silent movies. Dilly was also an ardent Nationalist and an active member of both Cumann na mBan and Sinn Féin, and it was through her involvement with the latter, that Michael first met her. They soon became friends and later their friendship turned into romance. She was to undertake many risky tasks for him and became very involved with his intelligence work. Frequently she accompanied Michael on dangerous missions. The handsome businessman, arm in arm with his pretty, well-dressed girlfriend – a perfect ploy that never aroused any suspicion from the RIC, Auxiliaries or the British soldiers.

Around 1918–1919 Susan Killeen, Dilly Dicker and Michael were all living in Mountjoy Street, about a three-minute walk from Vaughan's Hotel in Rutland Square. Michael was based at No. 44, which was known at that time as the Munster Hotel, owned by Miss MacCarthy, a staunch Republican from Kerry. Across the road at No. 19 Susan Killeen lived with her uncle Patrick and family, whilst further down the road at No. 30 Dilly lived with her father Edwin. Having two trusted and reliable friends as neighbours, as well as his landlady, was to prove very helpful to Michael as things began to develop.

An elderly resident of Mountjoy Street, remembered one such occasion. One evening there was a raid by the British army on No. 44, a hotel frequently used by the Republicans. Michael usually slept in the front bedroom above the main entrance. On this occasion as the soldiers stormed in, Michael quickly climbed out of his bedroom window and hanging on to the window ledge, with his feet resting the plinth above the front door, waited until the soldiers had finished their unsuccessful search. As they exited the building, Michael, heaving a sigh of relief, clambered back in.

Dilly often played the piano for him in the evenings whilst he scribbled away on his notepad at the table, sometimes falling asleep from sheer exhaustion. Occasionally he would hide in their loft when there was a raid on outside, or wait there until the 'all clear' from Miss MacCarthy at No. 44, across the road – she would rearrange her curtains as a signal. One of Dilly's most dangerous missions was to be smuggled on board the mail boat to England in one of the mail baskets, and to emerge in sorter's uniform. She was to extract any post for Whitehall, the British Secret Service Centre, and hide it about her person or in her handbag. She was then met by one of Michael's men in England, and the stolen mail was opened. On her return journey, she did the same, but this time extracted post destined for Dublin Castle or Secret Service men, working under assumed names and professions in the city. These were later steamed open under Michael's watchful eye. Michael's reward to Dilly was often a little trinket or sometimes a bag of sweets. Occasionally, when his busy schedule allowed, he took her out for an evening to a local dance or the theatre.

Sinead Mason was Michael's personal secretary from mid 1919 up until he was killed in 1922. Sinead was devoted to him as well as being a little in love with her boss. Despite his short fuse and tempers, they worked harmoniously together, she, knowing his every quirk. When he wanted sometime done *now*, he meant *now*! Michael, in return, had total confidence in Sinead and her work. She, like Dilly also took great risks and went on dangerous missions for him, often working a twelve-hour day or even longer.

Around 1920, Michael arranged for Sinead, along with her aunt, a Miss O'Connor, to move into 23 Brendan Road, in the Ballsbridge area of Dublin, just a few doors down from where his old friend Batt O'Connor lived. Batt still owned No. 23, having, around 1908, not only built all the houses in the road but also been responsible for its name. He originally wanted to call it 'St' Brendan's Road, after the well known Irish saint, but unfortunately had to compromise to 'Brendan', as the landowner was a Protestant.

Later, No. 23 was also used as a safe-house, after Batt constructed a secret room upstairs for Michael to sleep in. Around the same time, after the closure of the Dáil Loan in July 1920, Batt also had a secret cupboard built under the floorboards of his own house to hide the gold raised, some £25,000. Michael eventually arranged for the money to be smuggled out in a child's coffin. (Some years ago, the empty coffin was discovered in the vaults of a Dublin bank.) Michael was nearly caught by the British in No. 23. A list had been drawn up, by the army, of suspect houses in the Donnybrook area, and included both Nos 1 and 23 Brendan Road. Fortunately, just before the raid, a copy of the list fell into the hands of one of Michael's men, who quickly warned him of the impending danger. By 1920, it was too dangerous even for Batt to sleep in his own bed as the house was constantly raided. Despite the curfew, which at that time was at 10.00 p.m., Michael often called round in the evening, to see Batt and his family. Then, just before the deadline, both men would head off to their respective 'safe-house' sleeping quarters.

During one of the numerous raids on Michael's various offices Michael, frantically gathering up papers and documents to either hide in a secret cupboard or throw onto the fire before the soldiers arrived, tossed a diary to Sinead, saying she could keep it, destroy it or what ever. It was his 'Sligo' diary, a journal written while he was in Sligo Jail – she decided to keep it and many years later, her daughter had it published. The Collins family were very fond of Sinead Mason and hoped that Michael would marry her. She was sensible, intelligent and attractive, not unlike the Collins women. Around 1920 Michael sent her down to stay with his brother Johnny and his family at Woodfield for a holiday – to get away from the stresses and strains of Dublin, as the war began to take its toll on her health.

In May 1917, during the by-election campaign in South Longford, Michael first encountered the Kiernan family and met Kitty. Michael, his cousin Gearóid O'Sullivan and friend Harry Boland, who was already courting Kitty, stayed at the Greville Arms in Granard. The hotel, along with a grocery and hardware shop, bakery and undertakers were all run by the family – four sisters Christine, Catherine (Kitty), Helen and Maud and their brother Larry. They had lost their parents and twin sisters, through illness, whilst teenagers and had learned self-reliance at an early age. The Kiernans were staunch Nationalist and the sisters had all attended Pearse's school St Ita's, in the Ranelagh area of Dublin. During her time there Kitty became head-girl.

However, Michael first fell for the beautiful and vivacious Helen, although she was courting a local lawyer Paul McGovern. Around March 1918, Michael was again in the area and renewed his acquaintance with the Kiernan family.

At Legga, a few miles from Granard, Michael made a speech 'likely to cause disaffection' to the British. On his return to Dublin he was arrested by two 'G' men and after a brief hearing at Longford Courthouse, was remanded in custody and spent the following three weeks in solitary confinement at Sligo Jail, where he kept the diary, given later to Sinead Mason. Whilst incarcerated in the corner cell on the top level of the prison, Michael often gazed through the bars of his window, which offered a view over the prison wall, to the distant bulk of Knocknarea Mountain, reflecting on the destiny of both himself and his country.

Helen Kiernan came to visit him in prison, much to Michael's delight, and he persuaded her to stay in Sligo overnight, so he would see her again the following day. By now, Michael was besotted by her and on hearing she was soon to marry Paul McGovern, begged her not to marry him. Both he and her brother Larry were, for different reasons, unhappy with the idea of Helen marrying Paul. Frank O'Connor, a fellow Corkman and author of *The Big Fellow*, written in 1937, knew many of Michael's closest friends and was told 'that on the night before her wedding, Michael went to her hotel and pleaded with her not to go through with the marriage, and that during the wedding speeches he was so agitated that he shredded his handkerchief.'

Both Michael's and Larry's premonitions were correct. The marriage turned out to be an unhappy one, McGovern left his young wife in 1925, when their only son was three years old, leaving her to bring up the boy on her own. However, Helen being a resourceful Kiernan later ran a successful fish restaurant known as 'The Dive' on Duke Street, in Dublin's city centre. One of her grandsons is Barry

McGovern, the well-known Irish actor. Among the many roles he was to play both on the stage and screen, was as De Valera in the RTE film *The Treaty* in 1992.

In December 1918 a general election was called and Michael and his best friend Harry Boland were once again in Granard. Both men had managed to escape imprisonment, except for Michael's three week's in Sligo, whereas the majority of their fellow Sinn Féin leaders were not so lucky. Harry, just three years older than Michael, became involved at an early age in the GAA and the IRB. A Dublin man born and reared, he first met Michael around 1908 in London, when he was over there on GAA/IRB business. Both men fought during the 1916 Rising and were afterwards interned, Michael at Stafford Goal and Frongoch and Harry in Dartmoor Prison, where he was held until June 1917. At Dartmoor Harry met De Valera, for the first time. By late 1917, Michael and Harry were to meet up again, and by then, both were members of the Supreme Council of the IRB. After the 1918 general election, they were elected as Sinn Féin members of parliament, Michael for Cork South and Harry for Roscommon. However, both Harry and Michael, along with their fellow newly elected Sinn Féin MPs ignored the Westminster parliament in London and instead became TDs in the recently set up Irish parliament, Dáil Éireann at the Mansion House in Dublin in January 1919.

Since first meeting the Kiernans in 1917 Michael, along with Harry, became close to the family, staying frequently at the Greville Arms or sometimes visiting them at their holiday cottage. There they joined the girls and Larry on long walks in the beautiful countryside around Granard, or went boating on the nearby loughs – Gowna, Kinale and Sheelin. Occasionally, they would enjoy a game of tennis, Michael was a reasonably good player, having learned the rudiments of the game in England. The Kiernans were a social family and frequently held parties either in the drawing-room of the hotel or on a warm, summer's evening, in the large garden. Here they would spend the end of the day together, singing, dancing and reciting poetry, the latter being Michael's forte.

Harry and Kitty were sweethearts and by mid 1919 Harry was having serious thoughts about asking her to be his wife. Kitty – the middle class girl from middle Ireland – was an interesting woman. Pretty, rather than beautiful, smartly dressed and very modern in her taste, she took to using make up and enjoyed wearing revealing 'little black numbers' at the various dances and parties she attended. Kitty was also deeply religious, as many women were at that time, but independent-minded, bordering onto feminism. She spoke her mind and, like her three sisters, was a very good businesswoman.

She also took a liking to Michael and he to her, but because of her relationship with Harry and his friendship with Michael, Kitty kept her dealings with Michael platonic. However, this changed in June 1919, when De Valera having been recently 'sprung' from Lincoln Goal by the two friends, Michael and Harry, decided his presence was now needed in America to drum up support for the Irish cause – both financial and political. He asked Harry to accompany him, and he did so re-

Kitty Kiernan

luctantly, leaving his 'Dearest Kitty' in Ireland.

From then until August of 1922, Michael continued to come up to Granard and spend the odd weekend or night with the family, often accompanied by his cousin Gearóid O'Sullivan. Gearóid was taking a romantic interest in another of the Kiernan girls, Maud. She had originally been courted by Thomas Ashe, who had died in September 1917, having been force-fed. He, along with two other companions, Austin Stack and Fionan Lynch, had, at the start of their sentence in Mountjoy Jail, gone on hunger strike to gain political status. After Ashe's death, which was tantamount to murder by the prison authorities, the other two men, Stack and Lynch, along with another forty prisoners, were all released.

Gearóid and Maud eventually married in October 1922, a date that had been set for a double wedding with Michael and Kitty. In the wedding photo, a sad, heartbroken Kitty, dressed in black, is Maud's bridesmaid.

Whilst Harry was away in America, Michael's involvement with the War of Independence as Minister for Intelligence and Finance, as well as Director of Organisation, left him little time to pursue anything of a romantic nature. If he needed some female companionship he was still very friendly with Dilly Dicker, as well as having other women friends in Dublin.

Harry returned to Ireland briefly in May 1920 and, after boisterous reunion with Michael, headed up to Granard to see Kitty, hopefully to put their relationship on a firmer, romantic footing. Harry proposed to her, suggesting she should join him and have their wedding and honeymoon in America. However, Kitty did not take up this offer. Although she was fond of Harry, marrying him was another issue as she realised, that despite Michael's infrequent visits due to pressure of work, she was falling in love with him. Her feelings for Michael were different to anything she had felt for a man before. She would always look upon Harry as a good friend or brother, but never a lover. Kitty also knew that Michael secretly felt the same about her but, because of the 'triangular' relationship between the three of them, was too much of a gentleman to come between his best friend and his girl.

After the Truce on 11 July 1921, there was general feeling of euphoria across Ire-

The wedding of Gearóid O'Sullivan and Maud Kiernan on 19 October 1922 in the the garden of Walter Coleman's house at No. 3 Mountjoy Square, Dublin.
Front row from left: *Peggy O'Sullivan (Gearóid's sister), Donal O'Sullivan (Gearóid's brother), Julia O'Donovan, Seán Ó Muirthile, Maud, Gearóid, Jane O'Donovan (bridesmaid), Kitty Kiernan, Fr P. J. Doyle and Helen McGovern (sister of the bride)*
Back row from left: *unknown, Diarmuid Hegarty, Paul McGovern, Kevin O'Sheil, Dr Paddy Cusack (uncle of the bride), Seán MacEoin, Kevin O'Higgins, Paddy O'Sullivan (Gearóid's brother), unknown and Rev. P. Donnelly (the little boy in the front is Colman Doyle)*

land. Michael was even busier than ever. He travelled around the country, conferring with local IRA officers, checking their camps and equipment, as well as overhauling his intelligence network – not knowing when the Truce might break and the country plunge back into a war situation. However, he did find opportunities of seeing Kitty, and in August invited her down to Dublin for the Horse Show. It was during that time, in a Dublin at last rid of the horrors of war, that Michael and Kitty acknowledged their feelings for one another and Michael experienced the most intense and deepest love affair of his life. Over the next year, they corresponded with one another on a daily basis.

On the eve of his departure to England on 8 October 1921, a few days before his thirty-first birthday, Kitty became unofficially engaged to Michael. They were staying at the Grand Hotel (now La Touche) in Greystones, Co. Wicklow, which was later to become their 'bolt hole'. During the next few months and especially during the spring of 1922, when the political climate of Ireland was intense and Michael's life was even more exhausting, he found comfort and solace in Kitty's arms. He frequently travelled down from Dublin and joined her late in the evening – for something more than a long chat. Although she had little interest in politics, or understanding of what Michael was now involved with, she was a great comfort to him in other ways.

Michael and Kitty were two normal human beings, deeply in love with one another and planning to be married as soon as 'politics' would allow. Added to this, neither were in their first flush of youth, Kitty in her late twenties and Michael thirty-one. He was also a man of the world, and would have had by then a basic knowledge, even eighty years ago, of what is now known as 'safe sex'. Set against the background of those turbulent times and uncertain future, and taking into account the kind of people they both were, Kitty, a very passionate and vivacious woman and Michael, frequently being described as a 'virile' young man, it is quite obvious that their relationship was consummated whenever the lovers had a chance to be alone together.

Their daily correspondence also reflects their intense and overwhelming love for one another. In their earlier correspondence, Kitty was still fighting her Catholic conscience, knowing how Michael 'really wanted her' but later, realising that his feelings were genuine, and he had marriage in mind, she was happy to give herself to him both mentally and physically. Kitty's letters then became more revealing than Michael's, containing such lines as 'shuddering at the thought of her love for him' and 'wishing to be close to him to make sacred and profane love.' In another letter she said she went to bed early and lay awake thinking of him – 'madly, passionately in love with you, to use your own words' and later asking him 'not to be too rough or to hurt me when we are just playing, just fooling and a few other little ifs.' Just eight days before Michael was killed, Kitty wrote to him saying: 'she had taken a nice hot bath and then decided to have a dress rehearsal for him, first putting on her pink and mauve pyjamas, then a pink pair, then a nightie, which he liked the best and how in her imagination they had hugged one another and her mind was full of the loveliest thoughts and wishes that night, almost as good as if he were there.'

This 'dress rehearsal' was surely for their imminent wedding night. Kitty along with her sister Maud, who became engaged to Gearóid O'Sullivan in May 1922, discussed a double wedding, originally for 24 June, then postponed until 22 August. Both dates had to be cancelled, and the joint wedding put on hold, due to the political situation in the country and the start of the Civil War on 28 June 1922. By then, Michael and Gearóid were very involved with the renewed outbreak of fighting, this time between the anti-Treaty forces and the newly created Free State army, in which, by late June, both men had very prominent positions. However, this did not stop Kitty and Maud travelling to Paris that summer, to buy their wedding trousseaus.

It was also around the early summer of 1922, that Michael and Kitty found a house in Greystones, which they were planning to move into once they were married. 'Brooklands', a substantial late Victorian detached house, not unlike the Collins' new house at Woodfield, was just a few hundred yards up from the Grand Hotel, in Trafalgar Road. An aunt of Michael's also lived within a couple of minutes walk from the house, in Kimberley Road. She, I am sure, would have been very useful in future years, to help look after the large family Michael and Kitty were planning to have, after they were married!

Whenever Michael had the chance to visit Granard for the weekend or even a day to see Kitty, he would go. Otherwise, she would catch the train down to Dublin, sometimes staying at the Gresham or Shelbourne Hotels in Dublin's city centre, but usually Vaughans or Michael's old lodgings at the Munster Hotel in Mountjoy Street. Kitty even travelled over to London for a few days during the Treaty talks, to join Michael, along with her recently married sister Helen and husband, who were on holiday in London at the time. Michael took a few hours off from talks in Downing Street and escorted the two attractive and fashionable sisters, one on each arm, around the town. They went on a shopping spree, Kitty treating herself to an enormous hat, to which Michael commented, 'That the cart-wheel was bigger than the cart!' It was also during this visit that Kitty embarrassed Michael – wanting to be more intimate with him than the situation allowed.

When Harry Boland returned from America in early 1921, he soon realised things had changed between himself, Kitty and Michael. Later when their engagement was officially announced in early March 1922, Harry wished the couple 'Long life and happiness'. It is sometimes said that Harry took the Anti-Treaty side to spite Michael because of Kitty, but I feel this is very unlikely. He had spent the last year and a half with De Valera in America and became close to the man and his ideas. He also knew Michael had signed the Treaty as a 'stepping stone' towards a united Ireland, and was at heart as much a Republican as himself.

Kitty's engagement ring was a single stone diamond, costing £ 60 – nearly half a year's wages for a working man. Michael wrote to Kitty on Friday 10 February 1922, saying he was coming up for the weekend and asking her to meet him at Edgeworthstown station, the nearest to Granard. Also in the same letter he says 'By the way here's an item of interest – I have drawn a cheque for £60 today. Do you know what it is for?'

The following Monday 13 February, Kitty wrote Michael a short note:

> Ducky,
>
> Just a line. Will write later. I never felt so happy as I do today, T.G. So I hope you are likewise. Everything seems good and cheery and I feel oh! so happy. Bye bye.
>
> My love to you,
> Your own
> Kit

Kitty's birthday was sometime in February, and possibly it happened to fall that weekend or perhaps the couple chose a weekend nearest Valentine's Day, knowing Michael would not be around on the actual day, as he was attending meetings in London on the 14 February.

The events that finally led up to the Civil War, culminating in the deaths of Harry and Michael, were a terrible tragedy for Ireland. For Kitty, it was a very personal tragedy, losing a good friend in Harry, along with Michael, the only man she had ever totally loved and adored, within a few weeks of one another.

In 1925, Kitty met Felix Cronin, quartermaster general for the new National Free State army. He was a native of Lorrha in Co. Tipperary and had been active in the War of Independence and Civil War, taking the Pro-Treaty side, Felix was a great admirer, as well as a friend of Michael's. They married and had two boys. The first Felix, named after his father, was born in 1926, followed three years later by another son, Michael Collins Cronin – in memory of Michael.

In 1929, Felix left the army and joined Joe McGrath, another close friend of Michael's, to help run the then very successful Irish Hospital Sweepstakes. This involved at lot of travelling, sometimes to Britain or even further afield, to promote the sweepstakes tickets. Unfortunately, ten years later in 1939, the whole operation took a downturn due the commencement of the Second World War. Felix lost his job and eventually the family home, along with all their possessions, which included a painting of Michael by Sir John Lavery, that Kitty always kept either on an easel in the sitting-room, or sometimes hanging in their bedroom. Felix spent the war years checking turf lorries for Fuel Importers Ltd., and eventually became the company's general manager. However, despite their financial difficulties, he and Kitty sent both their sons to boarding school.

This slide into poverty was too much for Kitty to bear. She had always been relatively well off, enjoyed nice clothes and a good standard of living. In the early days of her marriage Kitty, along with her sisters, if not actually shopping, would hire taxis and ride up and down Grafton Street, the fashionable thoroughfare in Dublin' city centre, calling out to each other as they passed by. By 1940, Kitty's health began to fail and she spent the next five years in and out of nursing homes, finally dying in July 1945 from a progressive kidney disorder, nephritis, which was endemic in the Kiernan family. Both her parents, brother and sisters were victims of this disease and all died relatively young. Felix buried her as close to her beloved Michael's grave in Glasnevin Cemetery as was possible, and joined her sixteen years later in 1961.

During a recent meeting with Michael Cronin, Kitty's youngest and only surviving son, we briefly discussed his parent's marriage. He said that his mother was not an easy person to live with, possessing a quick temper and a sharp tongue. She was also very witty and assertive and, she told her boys later, that Michael Collins liked the way she spoke her mind to him. When Felix married his mother in 1925, he was aware that she was still very much in love with Michael and his 'presence' was always with them – as well as the painting. Unfortunately, his father became a heavy drinker in the early years of his marriage, a habit acquired from his days in the army and later the frequent socialising, which was all part of his job with the

Hospital Sweepstakes. However, he managed to give up the drink later and became a model husband and father. On discussing the Neil Jordan film *Michael Collins* and Julia Roberts' portrayal of Kitty Kiernan, Michael felt she did a very good job. The sharp tongue and assertive manner reminded him very much of his mother.

Whenever discussing Michael Collins and the many women associated with him, Hazel Lavery is the one woman most people assume Michael had an affair with. I suppose Hazel's legendary beauty, tall and slim, with a mass of auburn, curly hair and brown eyes, coupled with her reputation of being somewhat of a 'vamp' as far as men were concerned, helped promote this theory. He certainly did have a thing about women with red hair, and auburn is a reddish brown! When Michael, the handsome, charismatic and virile young leader of the Irish delegation re-entered her life in the autumn of 1921, their subsequent close relationship over the following year has always posed the question, was it platonic or otherwise?

As mentioned earlier Michael was first introduced to Hazel and her husband John through Moya Llewelyn Davies around 1913. Hannie and her younger brother Michael both socialised in the same London Irish circles as Moya, as well as being members of the London Branch of the Gaelic League. Although Hazel was born in the American city of Chicago, her family, the Martyn's, were originally from Galway. Her husband John, who was twenty-four years her senior, was born in Belfast in 1856, he was widower for many years and had one daughter Eileen. Hazel was also a widow, her first husband Ned Trudeau died suddenly a few months after their marriage in 1904. They too had one daughter Alice, born six months after her father's death. Although Hazel knew John Lavery before she married Ned, Hazel's mother had always been against her daughter's involvement with a man old enough to be her father. After Ned's death, Hazel's mother continued to live with her daughter and grandchild, but within a month of her death, Hazel and John married at Brompton Oratory in London, in July 1909. Their home, 5 Cromwell Place in South Kensington, was only a couple of miles from their friends the Llewelyn-Davies'. Around 1915, the Churchills were also to be neighbours, a friendship that grew when Hazel and John taught Winston, a budding artist, to paint. During the Treaty talks in 1921, this relationship was crucial. Hazel soon gained the reputation of being one of London's top society hostesses, mixing with the rich and famous, and in 1918 she became Lady Lavery, after her husband was knighted for his contribution as a war artist during the world conflict.

During the early part of the twentieth century, there was a burgeoning interest in Irish culture, music and language, promoted by the Gaelic League – an organisation that had been founded in Ireland at the latter end of the nineteenth century. Irish playwrights such as Bernard Shaw and Oscar Wilde were very popular at the time. Hazel and John Lavery were also involved and it is very likely that Hazel first met Michael and his sister Hannie at the Court Theatre, now the Royal Court, in Sloane Square, less than a mile from their home in Cromwell Place.

Hazel was impressed by the young man's knowledge and interest in Irish cul-

No. 5 Cromwell Place, London – home of the Laverys

ture, not only plays, but books, poetry and art. Being an artist in her own right, Hazel enjoyed the occasional visit to the London art galleries, possibly taking the young Michael along. It was this mutual interest in art and Irish culture that drew them together as friends and this friendship was renewed six years later, when Michael returned to London in October 1921, as one of Irish the plenipotentiaries involved in the Treaty talks with Lloyd George and his government.

Michael was more relaxed in the company of older women. He could be himself, keeping the relationship platonic, but at the same time using Hazel's influence to improve himself, both culturally and socially. Here was a woman ten years his senior, with a husband old enough to be his father, both well travelled and knowledgeable in the ways of the world. Their friendship was to have a great influence on Michael, helping to develop his cultural and artistic interests over the next three years, before returning to Ireland in 1916.

On his return to London in October 1921, Michael now a mature sophisticated and hardened man of the world, was to find solace in the Laverys' company. The ten years of living in London as a young man had also left their mark and in the autumn of 1921, the Lavery's introduced this very debonair, cultured young Irishman into London's top society and he was soon mixing with the rich and famous of the day. However, as the Treaty discussions became more arduous and exhausting, he preferred to spend an evening with them at their home, staying for dinner and relaxing afterwards in their library. He would sometimes accompany Hazel to the theatre, reliving his carefree youth, even if only for a few hours. It was also at Cromwell Place, that the men on the British side of the Treaty negotiations, such as Winston Churchill, Lord Londonderry and Birkenhead, were to meet Michael socially at dinner. Hazel played a central diplomatic role between both sides. And it was with Hazel, that Michael was to discuss his innermost fears and worries surrounding the Treaty talks, something he was unable to do with Kitty, as she had little understanding or indeed interest, in politics.

After the signing of the Anglo-Irish Treaty on 6 December 1921, Hazel continued as a 'go-between' for both the British government and the Irish delegation, some say even as a spy. Certainly, much of the correspondence and messages between her and Michael were in code, and could, on the face of it, have been taken for love letters. They, in fact, contained vital messages, either to the English cabinet or to the newly formed Free State Provisional Government. It was also around this time that rumours started to circulate that the two were having an affair. Hazel, despite being ten years older than Michael and married, was by now totally infatuated with him. She did nothing to dispel or deny these accusations – in fact, she openly encouraged them.

Fortunately, Kitty Kiernan never met Hazel until after Michael died and so never knew what a charismatic and beautiful woman she was. Kitty never suspected anything was going on between Hazel and her fiancée except once, a few weeks before Michael was killed, when she wrote, scolding him for not writing so frequently and asking him, 'Was there "someone else" in his life?' Michael's lack of writing was due no doubt to pressure of work, although it was around this time he found time to write his 'Cucugan' poem, dedicated to Hazel (see p. 44). In May 1922, the London press took a photograph of Michael with Hazel and John, with the caption 'M. Collins in Downing St with his sweetheart'. Michael wrote to Kitty the next day, explaining the situation and sending her on copies of the newspapers. She seemed quite amused by the whole episode!

In early 1922, Hazel decided to come over to live in Ireland for a while, renting a house in Greystones, Co. Wicklow, and leaving her husband John in London. Later that year both she and her husband returned to Ireland and stayed at the Royal Marine Hotel in Dun Laoghaire, or Kingstown, as it was then known, where Michael would occasionally join them for dinner. Hazel and John were also guests at a party Moya Llewelyn-Davies gave at her home in Furry Park, on Saturday 19 August, the evening before Michael travelled down to West Cork for the last time.

By this time there were many rumours circulating concerning an affair between Michael and Hazel, including one that they had recently gone away together for a weekend. Shortly before he died in August 2000 Michael's nephew, the late Michael Collins of Waterford, told me the truth behind this story:

About two weeks before Michael was killed in Beál na mBláth, Hazel tried to entice him away for a weekend but he refused to go, being a man of the world and realising what she had in mind. Also he was very in love with Kitty, and had enough problems with the Civil War and affairs of state, without any affairs of the heart, especially with a married woman. A blazing row ensued and the two parted company. They met once again, briefly at Moya's party at Furry Park, although Michael made sure he was not alone with Hazel during the evening. Just three days later, he was killed. Hazel was distraught when she heard the news of his death and she was particularly upset because he had died before she had the chance to apologise to him.

A couple of days later she was to appear in widow's weeds, visiting the mortuary chapel at St Vincent's hospital where Michael was laid out. It was there that John Lavery painted him for the last time – lying in state in his Commander-in-Chief's uniform, draped with the Irish tricolour. Hazel also attended Michael's laying in state at the City Hall, and at the funeral mass the following Monday held at the Pro-Cathedral was again dressed in widows weeds. Later that day, at Glasnevin cemetery, just after Michael had been buried, Hazel threw her rosary beads onto his grave but John quickly retrieved them as they were real pearls and anyone could have made off with them later. After the funeral and all the furore that had surrounded the event had finally settled down, Seán O'Connell, the soldier who had knelt beside Michael at Beál na mBláth and whispered the Act of Contrition into the dying man's ear returned to the grave and quietly buried her rosary beads.

Hazel remained friends with Hannie, Michael's sister, for the rest of her short life. She died in London in January 1935, aged 55, from myocarditis, an inflammation of the walls of the heart, brought on by an overdose of anaesthetic, having had a wisdom tooth extracted.

I believe the relationship between Hazel and Michael was a friendship of minds, certainly in the early days of 1913 to 1916. On his return in 1921, Hazel fell in love with him, as so many women who met him did, and Michael being a man of the world, would have delighted in 'winding her up' with poetry and flattery. However, she was ten years older than him, also married and both were Catholics, a religion that does not recognise divorce. Despite her many flirtations and admirers, Hazel and her husband were very devoted to one another throughout their married life. Michael was deeply in love with Kitty, and with his strong Catholic principles, would not have contemplated adultery, although perhaps the odd kiss or hug would have been excused!

I will let Alice, Hazel's daughter have the last word: 'My mother was always believed to have had an affair with Michael Collins. She never believed in affairs and she said, "Affairs are such shabby things; all that sneaking about by the back stairs." She was almost undersexed if you know what I mean, she had no interest. She liked things to be beautiful. Michael Collins was a very gallant hero.'

The other woman sometimes romantically linked to Michael Collins was Moya Llewelyn-Davies. Despite her Welsh sounding surname, Moya was Irish. Her maiden name was O'Connor and she was born in Blackrock, Co. Dublin on 25 March 1881. Moya, christened Mary Elizabeth, was the oldest, and only surviving daughter of James O'Connor – a Fenian and prominent member of the IRB. He was a journalist working on such papers as *The Irishman, The Shamrock, United Ireland* and editor of the anti-Parnell newspaper, *National Press,* for which he was imprisoned in Kilmainham Jail on a charge of treason in 1866. He later became the Member of Parliament for West Wicklow, a position he was to hold until he died in 1910.

Moya lost her mother Mary and four sisters in June 1890, when they were all poisoned having eaten polluted shellfish from the beach at Seapoint, less than half a mile along Dublin Bay from Blackrock. Moya survived because she had been sent to her room that day for misbehaving. This sad event was mentioned in James Joyce's *Ulysses* where Joyce comments upon 'poor Man O'Connor, his wife and children poisoned by shellfish on the Salthill shore.' They were all buried in Dublin's Glasnevin cemetery, as was James who died in 1910. After this tragedy, Moya's father, unable to return to the family home where his wife and daughters had perished within a few hours of each other, moved to Dublin city, taking Moya with him. A few years later, James O'Connor remarried, but, Moya and her stepmother were not compatible and at the age of eighteen, she went off to live with an aunt in London.

Having received a good education, Moya got a job with the British Civil Service in London and, through her work, she met Crompton Llewelyn-Davies in 1909, a vicar's son from Yorkshire. Crompton, thirteen years her senior, was a scholarship boy. He had studied law at Trinity College, Cambridge and, by the time he met Moya, had a flourishing legal practice in the city of London. He was very interested in social legislation and helped draft several Land Law Bills and the first Old Age Pension Act. For this, he was awarded a life peerage and was appointed Solicitor General to the Post Office, which at that time included Ireland, as well as England.

Crompton quickly fell in love with the tall, slim, fair-haired, blue-eyed young Irishwoman, and after a whirlwind romance, they married in 1910 and went to live in Kensington. They had two children, Richard born in 1912 and Kathleen about two years later. Around 1919, Moya decided to return to Ireland and from then until her husband died in 1936, was to have two homes – in Dublin and in London. After Crompton's death, she cut all ties with England, sold the family house in London and spent the rest of her life in Ireland.

Moya first met Michael Collins around 1910, through their shared interest in Ireland and Irish culture. She was keen in improving her Irish and joined the local Gaelic League. Michael was a fellow classmate and the two struck up an immediate friendship, due partly to her father's Fenian/IRB background. She also loved visiting the theatre, as well as enjoying music, literature and art associated with Ireland – all subjects they both shared a mutual interest in. During the next six years, leading up to 1916, the pair became good friends, despite their nine years age difference. Unlike Hazel, Moya had a great empathy with Michael's dreams for a united and free Ireland. She was one of the few to know that he was a member of the IRB in London, and was involved with the Irish Volunteers and the forthcoming Rising.

Crompton was fond of Michael too and was delighted that his wife had someone to share her Irish interests. Michael regularly went to dinner at their home in Campden Hill Gardens, Kensington which, around 1913, happened to be just a few minutes walk from where he and his sister lived at 28 Princes Road. Occasionally, Michael and Hannie would join them and the Lavery's for an opening night of a new play by Barrie, Shaw or Wilde in London's West End. All this was to end in January 1916, when Michael decided to return to Ireland and become involved with the Rising. Moya came back to Ireland three years later in 1919, buying Furry Park House, an eighteenth century country mansion with extensive grounds, near the then small village of Killester about three miles from the Dublin city centre. Although Moya and Michael did not meet during those three intervening years, they wrote regularly to one another.

On Moya's return to Ireland, Michael frequently used her house at Killester as one of his main 'safe-houses', staying at least one night a week or sometimes longer. Furry Park was also Crompton's residence in Ireland, as he was by 1919, Solicitor General to the General Post Office in Dublin, as well as being a close confidant and friend of David Lloyd George, the British Prime Minister at the time. Obviously, with Crompton's connections, Furry Park would have been the last place the army or the 'G' men of Dublin Castle would think of looking for the elusive Michael Collins.

Occasionally, Michael also used Furry Park as an office and a son of Moya's nanny, Annie O'Reilly (nee Hughes), related an interesting story about Michael and his mother. Annie was originally from Holyhead in North Wales and having left school went to work at a large hotel in Conway Bay. It was here around 1916–17 that she was to meet Moya, Crompton and their two children. They took an immediate liking to Annie and upon their departure, asked her if she would like to become their children's nanny. Annie took the job, and was employed both at the family's London home in Kensington, as well as their Dublin residence, Furry Park. Annie met her future husband at one of the regular dances organised by Moya for her staff and local residents, held in the basement of Furry Park House.

Annie also met Michael Collins at Furry Park. During his frequent visits to the house he usually kept his gun either on his bedside table, or if working in the study, beside him on the desk. As well as being the children's nanny, Annie also helped with light housework, such as dusting and always remembered Michael telling her, 'to never to touch the gun as it was loaded.' From then on, after that sobering piece of advice, Annie made sure she dusted around the weapon. Normally, in more dangerous venues, Michael and his men hung their guns outside the room they were in, on hooks below the window ledge, so in the event of a raid, no arms

Right: *Michael's revolver* and left: *Vinny Byrne's revolver*
[Collins Barrack, Cork]

would have been found on their person. However, at Furry Park, as a raid was extremely unlikely, Michael kept the weapon close by him.

As the War of Independence intensified, Moya's involvement in Michael's intelligence work grew. Through her husband, she was able to feed him information in connection with the British government and its plans for Ireland. She also physically helped him in various ways, smuggling arms around the country or acting as his 'girlfriend' as the following amusing story illustrates: Michael and Liam Tobin, a fellow Corkman, as well as chief executive of his intelligence network, along with Máire Comerford, another of Michael's couriers, and Moya were having tea in a restaurant near the GPO when a group of Auxiliaries burst in and started searching everyone. Michael, who was armed at the time, quickly slipped his gun to Moya under the table, who tucked it inside her knickers. He then whispered to the trio to follow him and holding up his hands, walked over to the officer in charge of the raid, saying they were in a hurry as the girls had to catch a tram. Both men were searched and then dismissed. The four, then walked coolly out of the restaurant and into the busy street, Michael taking Moya's hand and Liam, Máire's.

Moya was not only a very good driver but also had her own car. This, she frequently used to smuggle guns, buried in her suitcases and hat boxes, down to Cork, Kerry and Tipperary, for the men in the flying columns. On one such run, accompanied by Leslie Price, who was later to marry Tom Barry, they had a burst tyre. 'Fortunately' for them, a lorry containing a party of Auxiliaries passed by on the road. The soldiers, realising the women needed help, stopped and changed the tyre for the two 'helpless' females. Luckily for Moya and Leslie, the Auxiliaries never dreamt of searching a vehicle being driven by two smartly dressed women, especially one with a very pronounced Anglo-Irish accent. Moya's years of living in London had helped cultivate her voice, and this proved very useful on such occasions.

During the three years between 1919 and 1921, Moya occasionally met Michael to exchange messages or information, in the grounds of a neighbouring estate. These surrounded a large, decaying Victorian mansion, St Anne's, belonging to a Lady Ardilaun, who was part of the Guinness dynasty. As the women were good friends, Lady Ardilaun was happy for Moya to stroll through the grounds with her two children, who often accompanied her on these clandestine meetings. Moya would slip out of the back door of her Furry Park home and through another door in the wall of the old kitchen garden so she would not arouse any suspicion. This led her into the grounds of St Anne's, just a few minutes walk from the pavilion beside the artificial lake, where they usually arranged to meet. It was rumoured that Michael even had a safe-house just inside the walls of St Anne's, on the south-eastern corner beside what is now the junction of James Larkin Road and Watermill Road.

When Lady Ardilaun died in 1925, having no children of her own, she left the estate to a nephew who had little interest in his inheritance. The house and grounds fell into further decay and it was finally bought by Dublin Corporation in 1939. A fire gutted the house in 1943, but the grounds became a public park. The pavilion and artificial lake is still to be found, but the cottage, said to be used as a safe-house by Michael has long since disappeared.

Furry Park was Michael's 'safest' of safe-houses until March 1921. Unfortunately, during a raid on one of Michael's offices, rented under Moya's name, papers were discovered, revealing Moya's involvement with Michael and his intelligence network. The army then drove out to Furry Park to arrest Moya. Fortunately, on this occasion, no guns were found in the house, Moya usually kept them hidden in

St Anne's Park, Killester near Furry Park House

drawers, concealed only by her clothing, or in hat-boxes. However, personal letters from Crompton to his wife, strongly criticising the British government's policy towards Ireland, were discovered. According to Signe Toksuig's diary it was also around this time that British intelligence discovered it was Crompton had been responsible for passing on some of the names and addresses of the Cairo Gang, to Michael's intelligence network, which resulted in the Bloody Sunday killings and led to the demise of the British secret service in Dublin. Following the raid, Crompton was dismissed from his post as Solicitor General at the GPO, with a loss of his £2,500 salary a year. Moya, together with two other women, Eileen MacGrane and Patricia Hoey, were also at Furry Park and all three were arrested. Despite Crompton's friendship with Lloyd George, the three women were imprisoned for the next four months in Mountjoy Jail. The three were treated relatively well during their internment and were released soon after the Truce was declared in July 1921, with no charge being brought against them. Moya went straight back to London, to join her husband and two young children.

Michael also happened to be at Furry Park the night the army came to arrest Moya but luck, as usual, was with him and he managed to escape. As he heard the rumble of the approaching army vehicles along the drive, he dashed into the drawing-room at the back of the house and by pressing a lever at the side of the large marble fireplace, part of the mantelpiece and its surrounds swung open, revealed a secret passage. Michael climbed in, and quickly closing the entrance behind him, sped along the passageway that led under the house and out into the grounds of Furry Park, near an area that was known as the Nun's Walk. After the soldiers had finally left, having taken Moya and her friends away for questioning, Michael returned to the house to comfort her two traumatised children, and the following day, made arrangements for them to join their father, Crompton, in London.

Back in the early months of 1919, Michael had also been part of the Sinn Féin delegation sent to London, who had hoped to meet the American President Woodrow Wilson. Both Crompton and Moya had helped Michael with a draft submission to the president, requesting him to take up Ireland's cause for freedom from British rule. Unfortunately, the delegation never got the chance to meet President Wilson in London before he journeyed on to Paris to attend the Peace Conference. Later during the Anglo-Irish Treaty talks in the last quarter of 1921, Moya and Crompton were both residing at their London home Campden Hill Gardens, Kensington. Crompton had found another job, and was a partner in a well-known firm of London City solicitors, specialising in international law. It was around this time he assisted Michael with the technicalities of the Treaty along with drafting his various speeches.

Moya also assisted Michael by writing articles and pamphlets in support of Sinn Féin and the Irish fight for freedom, and later, in 1922, helped him write and compile his only book *The Path to Freedom*. She was also the ghost-writer behind Charles Dalton's (Emmet's younger brother) book, *With the Dublin Brigade 1917–21* and Batt O'Connor's, *With Michael Collins in the Fight for Irish Independence,* both published around 1929 by Peter Davies, a relation of Crompton. Moya was a very good writer as well as an Irish language enthusiast. Around 1933, together with George Thomson, she co-translated from the Irish, Muiris Ó Súilleabháin's *Fiche Bliain ag Fas* (Maurice O'Sullivan's 'Twenty Years A Growing') an autobiography of O'Sullivan's early life on Great Blasket, an island off the Atlantic coast of Ireland. Thomson and O'Sullivan both stayed with Moya at Furry Park whilst they were all working on the book.

During the Anglo-Irish Treaty talks in London from the middle of October to the beginning of December 1921, Michael, when time allowed, once again socialised with Moya and Crompton, as well as the Laverys. As with Hazel, he could discuss the ever more gruelling details and problems that arose daily from his talks with Lloyd George and the British cabinet. With Moya, a fellow Volunteer, he could confide his deepest worries, along with his hopes and plans for the future. This close relationship was to continue until his death in August of the following year. Of all his female friends, Moya's support and loyalty over the years was the most steadfast and endearing.

Moya recalled an interesting insight into Michael's plans for the future soon after his death:

> He was full of the re-making of Ireland and the thoughts he expressed were all on this subject. He outlined an immediate programme, and he then allowed himself to dream of a future Gaelic civilisation, and he felt his way towards the foundations on which is should be built. He spoke of the possibility of making our provinces – the provincial cities – living centres. He would like to see them given power and responsibility, in the hope that they would flourish, in art, and industry, and education, and become rivals with each other in a healthy competition.

Twenty years later, in 1942, Moya was to remember Michael thus:

> A man with a great and tender heart, who loved the beautiful in nature and in art as far as he had time or opportunity to find it. His friends who wrote about him have distorted him as much or more than his enemies.

In 1936 after her husband's death in London the previous year, Moya sold off the land around Furry Park house to boost her income. She left the house to her only daughter Katherine, and moved to Brookville, a large Victorian mansion near the then country village of Coolock. Around 1939, with the threat of another war, Moya decided to move down to Co. Wicklow buying Killadreenan House near Newtownmountkennedy. It was here she died On 28 September 1943, from the after effects of an operation for stomach cancer. During the last twenty years of her life, she kept herself busy with writing and was the arts and theatre critic for the *Irish Times.* Sadly, despite her past, Moya's remains now lie in an unmarked grave at Deans Grange Cemetery near Dun Laoghaire, Co. Dublin, just a couple of miles down the road from where she was born in Blackrock.

As with Hazel, Michael's true relationship with Moya will never really be known. But unlike Hazel, who made no effort to hide the fact that she was totally infatuated with Michael and openly encouraged the rumours that they were having an affair, Moya kept silent about the true circumstances surrounding her friendship with him. There was a story that Moya wrote a journal of her life and her relationship with Michael, which came to the notice of some of his old friends, who told Moya clearly, that it was never to be printed. The journal subsequently disappeared.

There is no proof if he ever had an affair with either, or both women – but this possibility only makes him a little more human, for at the end of the day he was not St Michael, just Michael! He was no different to any other man, a normal heterosexual human being with the same weaknesses, thoughts and desires. He may have achieved more in thirty years than most people achieve in ninety, and was very good-looking and charismatic, something he was conscious of from an early age. He put these attributes to good use throughout his life, and was aware that the majority of the women who worked for him in their various capacities were also a little, or more, in love with him. He was, however, a man of high principles.

Furry Park House

Moya Llewelyn-Davies

10

THE PRESS AND MICHAEL

Michael's involvement with the press and media came mainly after the Truce in July 1921. The rare photos taken of him from the period 1916 to 1921 were usually family ones. The two most popular are of him in his staff captain's uniform in 1916–1917, looking extremely youthful, and the studio portrait of him, taken in early 1917, in civilian clothes, soon after his return to Ireland from Frongoch. Incidentally, I was told by one of his grand-nieces that the uniform he was wearing in the 1917 photograph, happened to be the same one he wore in the GPO, which was quite badly burnt during the fighting. He also wore it at Thomas Ashe's funeral later that year. In the other photo, Michael is wearing a suit and sitting cross-legged, hand across the knee, as his late nephew Michael Collins of Waterford told me, to discreetly cover a tear in his trousers. Even at weddings where he was often the guest of honour, he would normally hang his head or stand behind someone, keeping a low profile for security reasons. The only photograph the RIC ever had of him was taken at the opening of the First Dáil in January 1919. A surly looking Michael stares out from the front page of the Police Gazette *Hue-and-Cry* of 24 December 1920, along with four others including Richard Mulcahy, under the heading 'Apprehensions Sought'. Michael, at the time, had a price of £10,000 on his head for his capture. This however did not stop him becoming a 'star' of the silver screen. Unfortunately, it was still in the era of the 'silent' movies, so unless someone, someday, discovers a long lost recording of his voice, we will never really know how Michael sounded.

Possibly the earliest occasion that Michael made a public appearance on film was at the funeral of Thomas Ashe in September 1917. On this occasion, after the Volunteers had fired three volleys over the grave, Michael in full Volunteers uniform stepped out from the crowd to address the mourners at the graveside. A very tearful and emotional Michael said these few words, first in Irish, then in English: 'Nothing remains to be said. That volley which we have just heard is the only speech which it is proper to make above the grave of a dead Fenian.' The funeral was filmed for propaganda purposes, with the Dublin Brigade of the Volunteers providing the cortege from the Pro-Cathedral up to Glasnevin cemetery. However, this was in the very early days of Ireland's struggle for independence, and Michael's presence then was of little interest to the British.

The next known time that Michael was to make an appearance on the silver screen was a few months after the opening of the First Dáil in the spring of 1919. De Valera, leader of the illegal Dáil Éireann, decided to raise £500,000, through loan bonds, to help establish and support the work of the new Dáil. Michael, as Minister for Finance had the task of setting this up and overseeing the whole operation.

Michael knew that placing advertisements in newspapers had little chance of success, as the British authorities would immediately close the papers down. He was, however, very aware of the new medium of film and with the help of his friend John MacDonagh, brother of Thomas, one of the leaders of 1916, decided to make a propaganda film to be shown around the country. They used the grounds of Patrick Pearse's school, St Enda's in Rathfarnham for the official launch, filming the entire sequence on the steps leading up to the main entrance. Many well-known people, especially women whose sons or husbands had died in 1916, were invited to be the first to buy the Loan Bonds. Amongst the guests were Mrs Pearse, mother of Patrick and Willie, Grace Plunkett, widow of Joseph, Mrs Clarke, widow of Tom, together with some of the recently elected Sinn Féin TDs of the new Dáil Éireann, such as Arthur Griffith and Joseph McGuinness. Michael was to feature in the short film, addressing the audience at the opening scene of the launch and then taking his seat beside Diarmuid O'Hegarty, Director of Communications. The block that was used to behead Robert Emmet a century before was used as a table, and a smiling Michael is seen greeting the donors and signing their bonds. Michael was aware that his natural, photogenic good looks would help promote the sale of the bonds. A few days later Michael's 'boys' were sent off to cinemas in various cities and towns around the country, with copies of the film, to be shown before the main feature. Occasionally a gun was used to 'persuade' the projectionist to carry out this task. The 'boys' then pocketed the film and vanished before either the RIC or the army could apprehend them. The film was also shown in cinemas around America, to raise funds over there.

An interesting point in connection with Michael's appearance in this propaganda film is that he is clearly seen standing addressing the audience, and later talking to the donors, both in profile and full face and yet this was never used, as far as we know, by the British intelligence, 'G' men or the army to find him. It was out of character for Michael to have appeared so openly in a photograph, let alone a film but it was made in the early days of the War of Independence, when Michael had not as yet become the 'thorn' in the side of the British. It is very likely the film was kept well hidden until after the Truce, when Michael's life of living on the run was finally over. The British never realised the young, handsome, smiling Minister for Finance, launching the loan, was later to be the mastermind behind Ireland's War of Independence.

The Truce between Britain and Ireland was declared on Monday 11 July and on 14 July, De Valera, along with Arthur Griffith, Robert Barton, Erskine Childers, Austin Stack and George Plunkett, went over to London to discuss peace terms with Lloyd George and his government. However, De Valera decided to leave Michael out of the delegation as he said he did not want him to become 'known' and photographed by either the British or world press. This did not make sense to Michael who, only a few months earlier, around January 1921, had been pressurised by De

Michael Collins at Croke Park with the Kilkenny hurlers, August 1921

Valera to travel to America, to continue his work in gaining support for the new Republic both financially and politically. Had he gone, Michael, like De Valera when he was in America, would have had numerous photographs, along with newsreel film footage, taken of him. It was in January 1921 that Michael realised it was a ploy of De Valera, to get him out of the country for a while. Michael was running things too well whilst De Valera was away campaigning in America for eighteen months, and on his return, Dev was jealous of Michael's success in organising Ireland's fight for freedom. There were a few bitter exchanges between the two men.

During the three months between the Truce and his involvement with the Treaty talks in London, Michael lost some of his anonymity. The Irish press and cameramen were following him around. The famous photo of him throwing the ball, along with Harry Boland at a hurling match on the pitch at Croke Park, is an example. Later in September, again at Croke Park, attending the All Ireland football finals with De Valera, Griffith and the Lord Mayor of Dublin, is another. Equally famous is the one of him posing with a new bicycle (see p. 23), dressed as a businessman, immaculate in shiny shoes, dark overcoat and light trilby, looking sternly into the camera. This photograph was taken during a visit he made to Pierce's Bicycle Factory in Wexford. Michael, who fought most of the War of Independence from the back of a bicycle, helped to advertise their latest model.

It was also around August–September of 1921 that two rarely seen photographs of Michael were taken. The first is of him during a picnic in Devil's Glen,

Michael with two Leigh Doyle children at a picnic in the Devil's Glen, August 1921

Co. Wicklow, standing on the footpath beside the river Varty, with two of Dr Brendan Leigh Doyle's children. The doctor and his family had been very good friends of Michael's for some years, and, during the Tan war, allowed him and his colleagues, to use both their Rathgar and Carlow homes, as safe-houses. The second photograph is of Michael as Minister for Finance, sitting at his paper-strewn desk, pen in hand. He appears to have been 'snapped', upon hearing his name called. Quite at ease, he raised his head, and turned to look at the camera. A small scar on the left hand side of his chin, the result of a childhood fall, can be seen quite distinctly in this picture, as it can to a lesser degree in his famous uniformed pose as the new Commander-in-Chief on the parade ground of Portobello Barracks, taken a year later. It was only because of the recent Truce situation that Michael allowed such personal photographs to be taken of him. Barely two months previously, had such photographs fallen into the wrong hands, his cover could have easily been blown.

The Minister for Finance at his desk

The talks, which continued through July until September of 1921, between De Valera and the British did not go too well. The Irish delegation soon realised that they were not going to get their longed for Republic, only Dominion Status. An oath of allegiance to the king would still have to be sworn, and that six counties of nine in Ulster would continue to be part of Britain.

In mid September, Michael decided to visit the north to try to persuade the Loyalists to support the idea of Republic and a united Ireland. Michael, accompanied by his friend Harry Boland, who had recently returned from America, travelled up to the ancient cathedral city of Armagh, where his constituents gave Michael a rousing reception – he was TD for Co. Armagh, as well as South Cork. This event was again filmed for posterity and shows a vigorous and dashing Michael, bounding onto a wooden platform, and addressing a vast crowd. He pleaded passionately to the Loyalists, asking them to 'join with us, as Irishmen, to come into the Irish nation, to come in and take their share in the government of their own country'. Michael's speech upset some of the local Orangemen and, as they were leaving, their car was surrounded by an angry crowd, who pelted it with stones, as it sped away.

On his return to Dublin, De Valera decided to send a new delegation to re-open talks with the British, and this time to include a very reluctant Michael, who along with Arthur Griffith was chosen to head the talks. Robert Barton and Erskine Childers were included again, plus two new members, George Gavan Duffy and Eamon Duggan. The press and media gathered at the quay to see off the new Irish delegation, who along with secretaries and other aides, sailed from Dublin on 8 October. Upon their arrival in London, the Irish community gave them a tumultuous welcome. On this occasion, Michael was to escape the glare of publicity and the press, by quietly travelling over the following day, accompanied only by his two bodyguards.

However, his anonymity in England did not last very long, and soon, not only the British, but also the world press were seeking him out. He faced a daily barrage of interviews and photographs, the press snapping at him whenever they got the chance. In the eyes of the press and the world he a very intriguing person. Because he was the man who master-minded the War of Independence and ultimately the man who got the British to agree a truce and to talks, everybody wanted to know what he looked like – was he some wild-eyed, evil looking ruffian? The fact that he was tall, handsome and very eloquent, took them all by surprise.

The talks between Britain and Ireland continued for two months, with Michael and the delegation making frequent return visits to Dublin for discussions with De Valera and other members of the Dáil on their progress, or lack of it, with the British. Michael also had numerous meetings with his colleagues in the IRB. Finally, in the early hours of the 6 December, after an ultimatum from Lloyd George of a resumption of an immediate and terrible war between the two countries, the Treaty was reluctantly signed. He had responded to Birkenhead's comment, 'I may have signed my "political" death warrant tonight', with 'Tonight, I have signed my "actual" death warrant.'

There are numerous photographs and even a short news film, made of Michael and his fellow delegates the morning after the signing of the Treaty. Both he and his fellow signatories showed signs of strain and exhaustion, and not the elation that better terms would have brought. Also, during the same day, a grim looking Michael is photographed and filmed, standing on the balcony outside Hans Place.

The delegation was all given a rousing send-off at Euston station by the London Irish. Michael was carried by exuberant supporters and lost his hat in the crowd. But their reception back in Dublin was very subdued, with De Valera and his colleagues extremely angry with the delegates for going ahead and signing the Treaty with the British, without consulting them first. However, after three weeks of stormy debates for and against the Treaty, except for an adjournment of a few days over the Christmas period, it was finally ratified on 7 January, with 64 for, and 57 against. A few days later, the new Provisional Government for southern Ireland was quickly set up, with Arthur Griffith as its president, and Michael as chairman. A serious and thoughtful Michael is seen sitting beside Griffith, surrounded by the pro-Treaty members of the new government – the event being filmed and shown at cinemas around the country. De Valera, after the ratification of the Treaty, resigned as president and stormed out of the Dáil. His fellow anti-Treaty supporters followed him, including Harry Boland, Michael's friend.

Whilst all this was happening, Michael was deluged with offers from various newspapers across the world for memoirs of his 'life on the run'. On the morning of 6 December, when the ink was hardly dry on the Treaty, the *Daily Express* had approached him for three exclusive articles concerning 'his adventures in Ireland when he was being sought high and low.' The payment offered was 'running into three figures'.

Then, in early January 1922, Mr F. D. Long, working for Sir Edward Hulton & Co, offered him £2,000 for his life story. They did not want 'political revelations' but 'the human story'. Later that same month M. F. McCartney, a publisher in London, contacted him and made him an offer of £10,000 for his 'Memoirs'. One thousand pounds on acceptance, a further £4,000 upon receipt of the manuscript and a final instalment of £5,000 upon publication!

The best offer came from the *New York World*. They offered Michael $25,000, cash, for the American and Canadian book and newspaper rights. The *World* syndicate at the time owned most of the newspapers in the United States and Canada, and had a vast circulation in both countries, together with a large Irish-American readership.

Michael turned down all these offers which, at the time, would have been enough for him to retire and live comfortably for the rest of his life. He did not have the time to undertake such a task as he had a new country to run, and many pressing demands on his time. He did somehow find the time to write one book between January and August 1922, *The Path to Freedom* – a collection of notes and speeches written by him over the years. Moya Llewelyn Davies helped him with the layout and text, and the book was published by Talbot Press in Dublin, shortly after his death in 1922.

I heard a rather strange story involving Michael and the press around the time of the post-Treaty negotiations in early 1922. It concerned a journalist, Patrick Murphy, who had previously worked for the *Freeman's Journal* in Dublin as a night reporter. He first met Michael one evening in Dublin around 1920, whilst they were both sheltering from a truck full of Black and Tans, patrolling the streets near Murphy's newspaper's office. The two men got chatting and when it was all clear, Murphy asked Michael back to his office for a cup of Bovril. The pair had just sat down to enjoy their drink when the Tans reappeared, bursting into the building, to raid the place, saying they were looking for a 'Big Fellow' and could he, Murphy, help them find him. Fortunately, the 'Big Fellow' had rapidly vanished and the Tans soon gave up the search and left. A distraught Murphy returned to his office, to discover both cups of Bovril were mysteriously empty! Suddenly the 'Big Fellow' re-appeared, clambering down from a skylight and onto the desk. On leaving, he remembered to thank Murphy for the Bovril!

By 1921–22 Murphy had joined the *New York Herald* as a reporter in London. He knew by then that the 'Big Fellow' he had met in 1920, was in fact none other than Michael Collins, the leader of the Irish delegation and now chairman of the new Provisional Government of Ireland. In early 1922, Murphy decided to contact him during one of Michael's frequent return visits to London – in connection with the setting up of the new Free State. Knowing Murphy personally, and remembering the 'Bovril' incident, Michael was happy to give an interview. He invited Murphy to come over and meet him at his London hotel. On entering the room, Murphy noticed a very expensive fur coat thrown on the bed. Michael, seeing the puzzled look on his face, quickly explained that it was a 'breaking-off' present for the girl he was going to marry. He then added that he had to break off the engagement because he did not want the girl to marry a corpse. He could not think what to give her until Murphy's paper, the *New York Herald*, sent him a cheque for £500, for a feature he had done for them. An even more puzzled Murphy then asked him what was he talking about being a corpse?

'That "they" wanted to get him and why shouldn't they get him. When he wanted anybody he got them, and he had trained the fellows who wanted him now. They could get him all right!' Michael replied.

I presume that 'they' were his ex-friends and colleagues back in Ireland, who were now against the Treaty and the new Free State.

Whether Kitty ever received the fur coat, is another story. There certainly is no evidence that Michael ever 'broke off' his engagement to her. In fact during his last few months, they wrote to one another nearly every day, as well as meeting when ever time would allow.

Michael was constantly in the public eye from the day he signed the Treaty until his death, less than nine months later. It was from around that time that he underwent a personality change – becoming far more serious, quieter and less fun-loving. He was at heart a soldier, not a politician and felt uneasy in the new role that had been thrust upon him. His honesty, implacable integrity and boyish charm did not suit his new position. Around Christmas of 1921, he also underwent a physical change, this time on his brother Johnny's advice, by shaving off his moustache. There was no need now for him to try to look older – the circumstances in which he found himself were doing that naturally!

One of his first duties on 16 January 1922 was to attend the handing over of Dublin Castle. In his role as Chairman of the new Provisional Government, a very dapper Michael in civilian dress is photographed leaving the castle, preceded by Kevin O'Higgins, then Minister for Economic Affairs. O'Higgins, although a reluctant 'yes' voter to the Treaty, was one of Michael's cabinet ministers.

Col Seán Clancy told me a rather amusing story about the handing over of Dublin Castle, where he happened to be on guard duty at the time. Col Clancy, born in 1901, had come up to Dublin from Co. Clare in 1918 to work as a clerk. He fought against the British forces during the War of Independence as a Volunteer in Michael's

Dublin Brigade. In early 1922, he was one of the first to join the new Free State army and was based at Portobello Barracks. Col Clancy saw Michael quite frequently during the six weeks he was Commander-in-Chief, although as Commander-in-Chief, he kept himself quite aloof and had no time for small talk with his men. After Michael was killed, Col Clancy marched in his cortege up to Glasnevin cemetery. He was to spend the rest of his life as a soldier in the new Irish Free State army until he retired in 1959. This is his memory of the castle handover:

'It was a cold bleak day and Michael and his entourage arrived a few minutes late in an old LSE taxi. They had been delayed due to a rail strike, Michael, having journeyed down from Granard by train earlier that morning, after spending the weekend with Kitty Kiernan. He was met by General Macready and other officials all dressed either in uniform or morning dress. The British officer who was overseeing the formalities commented on Michael's lack of punctuality, to which Michael chuckled and said: "You've been here seven centuries, what bloody difference does seven minutes make now you are leaving!"

'After the ceremony, the Lord Lieutenant went to shake Michael's hand saying, "I'm delighted to see you Mr Collins". To which Michael laughed and replied, "Like hell, y'are!"'

During those turbulent, final few months of Michael's life, he was constantly being photographed and/or filmed. Under the terms of the Treaty, a general election had to be held and the Treaty put to the electorate. The rumblings of the anti-Treatyites started to manifest in the early months of 1922. As the new Free State army took over the barracks from the departing British, the IRA brigades began to split between pro- and anti-Treaty. To try to avert a possible Civil War, the Republican and Free State leaders got together and signed a pact on 20 May. The 'Pact' election, as it became known, was held three weeks later on 16 June. One of the last known photos, and films, of Michael sitting with De Valera and Harry Boland, was taken that day in the gardens of the Mansion House, just after the pact agreement had been reached. In the film version one can see a smiling Michael, chatting and laughing with Harry, possibly one of the last occasions the two friends were ever to be seen together again in public.

As well as frequent visits to London, usually travelling overnight to save time, to sort out various problems that had developed since signing the Treaty with the British government, Michael also toured around Ireland, north and south, addressing huge crowds and giving his views on the Treaty and the Articles of Agreement. His meetings, held at College Green in Dublin and later in Cork city, the day before the election, drew immense crowds, together with the press and film-makers. His visit to his hometown of Clonakilty in West Cork, shortly before the election, was filmed for propaganda reasons. Here, an ebullient Michael, trilby-hatted, raincoat billowing, is seen energetically greeting people, chatting to old folk, shaking hands, smiling with the locals, and ruffling the hair of a small boy. In another sequence, hat pushed back, he is seen laughing and joking with a farmer. Later on, standing in his open-top touring car, outside O'Donovan's hotel in Clonakilty's main street, he is filmed, earnestly addressing an enthusiastic audience – the hero's return. Joan Bunworth, daughter of Johnny Collins and only surviving niece of Michael, who actually remembered him as a small child, said, 'That he was always the Clonakilty boy.'

Although he was Commander-in-Chief of the army for only six weeks, some of the best-remembered images are of him resplendent in his uniform. Uniforms are usually becoming on any man, but even more so on a man like Michael. The press descended on him the day he became General Collins, dressed in an ill-fitting uniform, with a button missing from the breast pocket. The well known photograph of him striding across the parade ground at Portobello Barracks with the little lad Alphonsus Culliton a few paces behind, is another. Alphonsus, originally from Ireland, had moved to England with his mother and stepfather in whose hands he was to suffer years of abuse. Eventually, at the age of fourteen, Alphonsus stowed away on a ship bound for Dublin and was nearly killed in the opening shots of the Civil War. He was brought to the Portobello Barracks and Michael, who always had a soft spot for children, took him under his wing, and decided to make him the first mascot for the new army.

However, it was at Griffith's funeral that Michael was to make his greatest visual impact on the public. Not only was he now the head of the new Provisional Government but also of the new Free State army. Michael marching beside Mulcahy, Minister for Defence, tall, handsome and dashing in his new green general's uniform, with the gold bars on his epaulettes, struck a cord in every observers' heart. However, his demeanour was grim, not only was he upset and saddened by the loss of his old friend Griffith, but the numerous worries of state and the ongoing Civil War were very much on his mind. A good part of the funeral was filmed and the cameramen panned in on Michael whenever possible, carrying the coffin, talking to his colleagues and later in Glasnevin standing head and shoulders above most of the crowd beside Cosgrave as he delivered his panegyric at the grave.

There is a photo of Michael outside of the Pro-Cathedral just after Griffith's funeral service, where he appears to be mobbed by a crowd of women who seem to be looking for his autograph – many of whom are determinedly pushing through the throng to get closer to the already hemmed in figure. An extremely vexed Michael appears to be shouting over the crowd at one of his men, to help him out of the situation!

It was also during the funeral of Arthur Griffith that some of the best known 'in profile' photos of Michael were taken, where he appears to be consciously displaying his striking jaw-line, as he glances at the passing cameramen. These pictures include what has since become the most famous Michael Collins image of them all.

Michael, resplendent in uniform, gloved hands punched into each other before him, handsome profile swung to the right. A pose to be immortalised in Leo

Whelan's frequently reproduced 1922 painting – the original later to hang in the hall of Leinster House, home of the new Irish government.

Michael Collins at Arthur Griffith's funeral, 16 August 1922

11

MICHAEL AND THE KERRY BLUE TERRIERS

It hardly seems possible that Michael, whilst being the mastermind behind the War of Independence, as well as Minister for Finance, Intelligence, Operations, and some would also say 'general mayhem', would find the time to take a very keen interest in the uniquely Irish Kerry Blue Terriers. These fierce, loyal little dogs, originally from Co. Kerry found a place in Michael's heart and affections. Although he was unable to keep a dog himself, due to his precarious lifestyle, I feel sure that had things turned out differently and he had eventually married Kitty and settled down to a normal life, one of their first priorities together would have been to acquire a couple of these Irish terriers as pets.

Kerry Blues are a very old Irish breed, but according to legend, their origins were either the result of a Russian black terrier or a Spanish long-haired 'puddle' or poodle mating with a local Kerry terrier. The Russian terrier was supposed to have escaped from a ship anchored in Kenmare harbour in Co. Kerry and mated with a local Irish soft-coated wheaten terrier. Whereas the Spanish poodles arrived in Ireland in 1588, after half of the Spanish Armada was sunk during a terrible storm off the coast of Kerry. Some of the dogs aboard the sinking vessels, managed to swim ashore, and later mated with the local terriers in the coastal villages

For the first eighteen months of their lives their coats, which are soft and silky resembling astrakhan, are black. It then changes to blue-grey and, like the West Highland Terriers, does not moult. An extrovert at heart, the Kerry Blues are a fiery spirited animal, determined but adaptable. An ideal pet, kind with people and very loyal to their owners, they make excellent guard dogs as well as good working dogs. Over the centuries, they were used for hunting, ratting, guarding sheep as well as protecting their owners.

The Kerry Blue, or as they were known in Dublin around the turn of the century, the Irish Blue Terrier, were a pedigree breed and had to be registered through the English Kennel Club before the animal could compete at dog shows. The owner was charged the princely sum of two shillings for this privilege. At that time, they were shown in their 'natural' state, unlike today when they are trimmed to look not unlike a poodle.

Around 1920, a breakaway Irish Blue Terrier Club was founded, and included Michael and his friend Dr Oliver St John Gogarty amongst its members. Michael later became its president. They decided to hold a dog show of their own outside the jurisdiction of the English Kennel Club. Despite the curfew across Dublin, and the subsequent risk of arrest or even death, if caught out on the streets after dark, it was held on the evening of 16 October 1920, Michael's thirtieth birthday. The

Bessie – a present-day Kerry Blue

venue was Longrishe Place in the Summerhill area of Dublin and Michael competed with his dog 'Convict 224', which won first prize. Dog and master were awarded the Wyndham Quinn Perpetual Cup, named after a fellow member of the newly formed club, Captain Wyndham Quinn who resided at the Vice Regal Lodge in Phoenix Park. Both he and the Under Secretary for Ireland, Sir James McMahon, who interviewed Nancy O'Brien for her top-secret job at the GPO, also attended, showing their dogs that evening. Their love and interest in the Blue Terriers obviously meant more to the two men than politics.

The Wyndham Cup, which is also known as the Collins Cup, is still awarded to 'Best of Breed' at Kerry Blue dog shows to this day. Michael's name, along with his dog 'Convict 224' is engraved at the top of the cup, as they were the first to win this prestigious award. The following year 1922, it went to a Thomas Gilmore with his terrier 'Shelbourne Rose'.

At the Longrishe Place show, Michael gave his address as Inchicore, Dublin, where one of his aunts resided and where he first stayed for a couple of weeks having arrived in Dublin from London in January 1916. His aunt, Mrs Donovan, lived at No. 3, St Michael's, Sarsfield Road, and it is likely she and the family cared for the dog or dogs. Another of Michael's dogs was called 'Danny Boy' obviously named after one of his favourite Irish ballads, the 'Londonderry Air'. He also owned another called 'Kitty', which I assume was named after his fiancée, Kitty Kiernan.

During the period between 1917 to 1921, despite the growing hostilities between the British and Irish, there were never any real problems at sporting events such as dog shows, horse races, etc. and especially at the RDS (Royal Dublin Society) showground in Ballsbridge, which was and still is, used to host the top Irish national sporting and social events. During the early days of the Truce around August 1921, Michael along with his dog 'Danny Boy' attended a show at the RDS and won first prize for best of breed. Amongst the spectators at the time were British soldiers as well as 'G' men, but due to the Truce no attempt could be made to apprehend him.

Michael had always liked and taken a keen interest in the Kerry Blue terrier and obviously knew someone who was involved in promoting and breeding them. Over the years (1917–1922), he was in the habit of giving a dog as a gift to various friends. One of the first recipients was Dulcibella, sister of Robert Barton, who lived with her brother and his family at Glendalough House, Annamoe in Co. Wicklow. Writing to Michael in May 1918 she said that Jim, the dog he had given her, 'spent most of his time tearing around the garden chasing the cat or sleeping on her bed.'

Michael frequently stayed with the Barton family, using their house as a base for touring around the Wicklow countryside on his bicycle to collect money for the Irish National Aid Association – set up in Dublin to help the widows, orphans and dependents of those killed or imprisoned after the 1916 Rising On his return to Dublin in January 1917 Michael was appointed secretary. He continued to use Glendalough House as a base for touring around the area later in 1919, after the launch of the Dáil Loan. An old estate worker, whose father had known Michael around that time, remembered him returning to the house one evening with what he thought was £2,000 in gold sovereigns in his saddlebag. On counting the money, he found it was nearer to £4,000!

Another recipient of a Kerry Blue was his best friend Harry Boland, who, on his visit to the States was given not one, but two dogs, as companions. In those days, there was no such thing as quarantine! Hazel Lavery was another proud owner, Michael presenting her with a dog during one of his frequent return visits to London in 1922. She called the animal 'Mick' and it was rumoured that the only person it did not attack, other than Hazel, was himself.

Around the same time, Michael also had Lord Birkenhead on his 'gift' list for a Kerry Blue. Birkenhead, or F. E. Smith as he was known, was a brilliant lawyer and one of Lloyd George's right-hand men on the British side during the Treaty talks. Although originally an adversary of Michael's and his dream of Irish freedom, Birkenhead soon warmed to his honesty, integrity and plain-speaking and the two men became good friends.

Having mentioned previously that Michael would have been unable to keep a dog himself, due to his precarious life style, it is also possible that as well as using his aunt's house in Inchicore, he could have also kept a dog at either of his two main safe-houses, Batt O'Connor's and/or Julia O'Donovan's. Both houses were situated in the quieter suburbs of Dublin, with enclosed back gardens and each had children available to exercise the animals without causing any suspicion. Moya Llewelyn Davies could have been another possibility as her house in Killester was surrounded by extensive grounds. But unlike the O'Connors and O'Donovans, Moya was occasionally absent from her Dublin residence, visiting London to attend to family matters but she had a housekeeper, as well as several servants, who could have easily taken charge of the animal whilst she away. Moya was very fond of animals and in particular cats and dogs. After she left Furry Park in 1936, she started the first 'rest fields' for horses and donkeys, possibly one of Ireland's earliest animal sanctuaries in the grounds of her house 'Brookville' near Coolock village. Later, in 1939, when she moved down to Killadreenan in Co. Wicklow, Moya continued to use the extensive grounds of her new home for the same purpose.

On a sadder note, probably the last dog Michael ever stroked before he was killed, was a Kerry Blue. On that fateful evening of 22 August 1922, after having left Lee's Hotel, now the Munster Arms, Bandon, where Michael and his entourage had stopped for a brief meeting, they then headed back to Cork via the Crookstown road, the only one passable at the time. As the convoy drove up the steep Kilbrogan hill, just outside Bandon, they saw a woman walking down the hill, accompanied by a Kerry Blue dog. Upon recognising his favourite breed, Michael ordered the driver to stop, and opening the car door, bent down to fuss and stroke the animal, whilst briefly explaining to its owner how fond he was of dogs, especially the Kerry Blue breed. Less than an hour later, Michael was killed at Beál na mBláth.

The popularity of the Kerry Blue, especially around the Dublin area, was to increase dramatically from around the time of the Truce up to the beginning of the Civil War. It was during this period that Michael, along with his personal interests, was increasingly in the public eye and included his involvement and promotion of the Kerry Blue terrier to be adopted as the national dog of the new Free State – just as the bull-dog was to England. It soon became fashionable to be seen with one of the Big Fella's dogs around the streets of the city and after the Irish Kennel Club was finally established in early 1922, the Kerry Blue was established as Ireland's national breed.

12

HOWTH

Forming the northern boundary of Dublin Bay, just ten miles from the city centre, lies the charming fishing village and headland of Howth or Benn na hEadair. Howth, which originally was named 'Hovud 'meaning' headland, was occupied by the Vikings who first landed in Ireland during the seventh century. Connected to the mainland by a narrow isthmus of sandy land, the peninsula consists mainly of rocky terrain and heathland and is bounded on three sides by sheer cliffs. From its three highest points Sheilmartin, Dun Hill and the Summit, magnificent views can be had across the bay to the city and up to the Dublin and Wicklow mountains. From its north side, on a clear day, can be seen the distant panorama of the Mourne Mountains, and just about a mile out to sea, the small uninhabited island of Ireland's Eye. Although the population and the amount of housing has increased considerably since Michael first visited the peninsula, it is still well known for its magnificent array of wildflowers to be found in its hedgerows, heathlands and cliffs. Numerous seabirds and waders, together with the local grey seals, are to be found along its shores, usually seen swimming around the harbour area, searching for fish.

In Michael's day there were several small farms scattered around the peninsula and the fields were used mainly to graze sheep and cattle. Most of these have now been taken over for housing and the few fields that have survived, graze only horses or donkeys. However, fishing was, and still is, part of daily life in Howth, along with tourism. Ninety years ago, most tourists would have arrived by train or electric tram, courtesy of the Great Northern Railway Company. They would have stayed in the fashionable hotels such as the St Lawrence, Claremont, Fortin's or the Royal, now renamed the Bailey Court – the only one still surviving as a hotel in Howth. It was in front of Butson's Hotel – now the Pierhead – that the Volunteers were photographed with their bicycles, having off-loaded the guns from the *Asgard* before marching back to Dublin in July 1914. There were also numerous boarding houses and tea-rooms, as well as public houses such as the Cock and the Abbey, both very popular pubs to this day.

Possibly one of Michael's first visits to Howth was in July 1914, where as a member of the IRB he was to help oversee the *Asgard* gun-running. Just three months earlier in London, along with his cousin Seán Hurley, Michael had enrolled in the No. 1 Company of the London Irish Volunteers, as part of the IRB's plan to infiltrate and control the Volunteer movement. On the day the *Asgard* sailed into Howth harbour, there was an interesting photograph taken at the time, near the entrance of East Pier with the Clontarf & Howth Electric Tram Station and Parcel Office in the background. A taxi is seen speeding away, loaded with some of the guns from

Asgard gun-running at Howth, July 1914

the *Asgard*, partially blurred in the camera shutter as it roars past a cheering crowd of onlookers and volunteers who line either side of its route. Amongst the ecstatic throng is Seán Heuston, later to become one of the leaders of the 1916 Rising. Also, watching the proceedings, back to the camera – tantalisingly – is the familiar figure of a burly young man in an overcoat and trilby. Could this be Michael Collins? In another photograph taken on the same day, De Valera can be seen quite clearly, along with his fellow Volunteers, marching past the wall surrounding Howth Castle demesne, which is still part of the main Howth road to the city, en route back to Dublin.

Tim Pat Coogan made an interesting comment about Michael's presence at the *Asgard* gun-running in his biography of Collins. Tim Pat attended a funeral of a friend in Howth, on the same day as the state funeral of Erskine Childers. His father, also Erskine, had, along with his American wife Molly and her friend, Mary Spring Rice, been responsible for bringing in the rifles to Howth from Germany, using their yacht, the *Asgard*. Whilst walking around the harbour, Tim Pat met two old men who had been watching the planes flying into Dublin airport, bringing the foreign dignitaries over for the state funeral. One of them, turning to Tim Pat said reflectively, 'you know, I was here the day his father sailed in with the guns. Michael Collins put me up on his shoulders so I could see.'

When Tim Pat quizzed him, the old man said, 'No, I knew him well. He used to stay up there sometimes with some of the lads. There was a house up there,' he continued, indicating towards Church Street and the police barracks, 'and there was good-looking girls living in it. The lads used to be after them. He was fine-looking fellow himself, God rest him.'

The 'good looking' girls were, amongst others, Michael's second cousin Nancy O'Brien along Susan Killeen and Dolly Brennan, who from 1914 to 1917, lodged with Mrs Quick at No. 1 Island View House, Harbour Road – now a restaurant known as 'Hell's Kitchen'. Mrs Quick was a staunch Republican and very sympathetic towards the idea of Irish independence. Although by 1919, the girls had all moved to Dublin to live, they were still friendly with their old landlady, and Michael got to know her during his brief visits to Howth from 1914 to 1916. It was here that Michael, along with Dilly Dicker, and some of his boys, would steam open the mail, especially that destined for Dublin Castle and redirect it or not, as the case may be. Also, it is rumoured, that the cottage rented by the Yeats family between 1880 and 1883, along the Balscadden Road, originally Kilrock Road, just outside of Howth village, was another location used for 'sorting' the Royal Mail.

No. 1 Island View House

Although the *Asgard* gun-running, which took place on 26 July 1914, is fairly well documented, I have been told that there were many other landings organised through the IRB to help arm the newly created Irish Volunteers. Howth harbour was frequently used for this purpose, being conveniently close to Dublin city, but at the same time quiet and remote.

In fact, the guns that were landed in Kilcool, Co. Wicklow, also in 1914, had a Howth connection. Eoin McNeill, a professor of Irish, and founder of the Irish Volunteers in November 1913, lived in the village, at a house called 'Aberdelgie' near the station. He was also very friendly with the local fishermen, who were happy to help the cause of Irish freedom in anyway they could. McNeill arranged for a consignment of arms from Germany, to be smuggled aboard the yacht *Chotah*, belonging to the Dublin surgeon, Sir Thomas Myles. At a pre-arranged time and position, near the Kish Bank, Myles along with his friend, James Creed Meredith, met with the Howth fishing-boat *Nugget*, owned by the McLoughlin brothers. Incidentally, the *Nugget* was the first fishing boat in Howth to be fitted with an engine. Also on board were some of McNeill's Volunteers to assist with the transfer of the guns. Later that day the *Nugget* landed at Kilcool Strand, and its cargo of 600 rifles with ammunition was safely delivered to Cathal Brugha and Seán T. Kelly, together with a unit of Volunteers.

Michael was enchanted by Howth itself, the rugged coastline and cliffs reminding him a little of his own beloved West Cork. Later, during the War of Independence, he realised its potential not only as a base for gun-running but, being just ten miles from the city centre, an ideal place for other more subversive activities. Sorting through the post intercepted by his agents on the mail boats was one, another, being a perfect location for 'very' safe-houses. He had the use of at least three in Howth during that period.

I recently discovered that Michael had relations called Butterley living in a house known as 'Foil-trá', in Church Street, Howth, around the 1914 period. He

Foil-trá

would have obviously stayed with them in the July of that year, whilst overseeing the gun-running, and later, during the War of Independence. 'Foil-trá' was an ideal 'safe-house' for Michael, as it was a large four storey building on two levels. The front faced onto Harbour Road (now part of Beshoff's), and the rear of the building, Church Street and Dunbo Hill, which was the beginning of the old Dublin Road, cutting through the woods and fields surrounding Howth Castle. It was also just across the road from the RIC barracks.

Bridget Josephine Collins came up to Dublin to live, having first helped to run the new creamery at Mitchelstown, Co. Cork. Bridget met and later married a wealthy businessman, Jeremiah (James) Butterley from Baldoyle, who, with his brother Joseph of Church Street, Howth, ran a very successful coal merchant's business at Waterside, Harbour Road, in the village. The beach beside West Pier, where the fishing boats were painted and tarred, was known as Butterley Strand. The passageway and steps leading down from Church Street to Harbour Road, beside the Butterley's house, were called Butterley's Steps. The brothers also owned a fleet of ships, as coal had to be imported into Ireland then, as it still does today. Just as an aside, I heard there was a popular saying during the War of Independence – 'Burn everything British, except their coal!' Joseph and his family were all involved with the *Asgard* gun-running in July 1914, as were most of the residents of Howth. Later in May 1920, through his maritime connections, Jeremiah arranged to have Harry Boland smuggled aboard the White Star Liner *Celtic*, which was docked in New York harbour. Harry worked his passage back to Ireland from America as a stoker, along with two of Jeremiah's cousins. At the time, Harry's visit to Dublin was kept quiet, as it involved secret meetings with Michael, his intelligence organisation and the IRB.

In was during this secret return visit to Ireland Harry Boland, along with his brother Ned and Michael travelled out to Howth and hiring a boat, from the slip-way next to Mrs Quick's house in Harbour Road, crossed over to nearby Ireland's Eye, for the day. Having explored the small island and eaten barnacles found cling-ing to the rocks, they made a fire from the driftwood scattered along the only ac-cessible beach, on the west side. Passing around a small flask of Jameson whiskey and enjoying the odd cigarette, the men discussed their hopes and dreams for Ire-land's future. Harry's plan was to organise the Irish race all over the world for the last phase in the struggle for freedom, and Michael encouraged him to press ahead with his ideas. Later that evening Saturday, 6 June, Harry wrote a tribute to his old friend in his diary. 'Ireland has the man of a generation … He stands out as the greatest force of the movement'.

Michael used to occasionally stay in another house just a stones throw from the RIC barracks. This was a cottage at the end of Evora Terrace, belonging to the O'Rourke family, where from the back garden, one had a very good view of the barracks and the harbour. The row of cottages had the added advantage of having one long, common attic, the dividing walls between each property only reaching as far as the ceiling. This was ideal if Michael wanted to hide or make a quick get-away, climbing into the attic of No. 6 and escaping out of the back window of No. 1. He always slept in the small bedroom at the front of the cottage, and was theref-ore the first to hear anyone approaching the front door. Years later, Mrs O'Rourke, when speaking about Michael, always referred to him as being: 'The best man in Irish shoe leather'.

Michael was, by 1919, friendly with two brothers James and John O'Brien. John was one of the many local farmers on Howth who used to supply milk to the village. His farm was situated in what is now Kitestown Road, but was then known as Bakers Lane. John had a hay-shed in one of the fields behind his farm, and Michael occasionally used this if things got desperate. His brother James lived in a small, remote cottage, known as 'Heather Cottage' situated at the foot of East Moun-tain, a short distance from the rugged cliffs that sweep down to the sea on the east side of the Howth peninsula. From its garden, one could look out across to the sea. Its remoteness and beauty appealed to Michael and he would usually make James' cottage his 'Howth' safe-house. Sadly this picturesque little place is no more and the site is now being developed for yet another of Howth's mansions. I was for-tunate to gain access just before building works commenced in the autumn of 2002, and also discovered the overgrown footpath leading down from the cottage to the main cliff path that skirts the east side of the peninsular from the Bailey lighthouse to Howth village. I am sure Michael would have used this pathway as a shortcut down to the village, enjoying its solitude and beautiful scenery.

This pathway led down to the end of Balscadden, or Kilrock Road, as it was known in Michael's time, a rough limestone track, eventually leading into Howth. Michael had another safe-house here, 'Cliff Cottage', belonging to the Carmody family. In July 1914 two of the sisters, Nora and Bridget, active members of Cumann na mBan, had been responsible for giving the 'all clear' to the *Asgard*, to bring in the guns into Howth harbour. Having got word that there were no soldiers in the locality, the two women climbed to the top of the cliffs, above their cottage situated to east of Balscadden Bay, and signalled to the yacht, by using a large white sheet.

It was also at Cliff Cottage, in early December 1921, that Michael left, over-night, the final draft of the Treaty. Michael, together with the other delegates, tra-velled over to Dublin for a meeting with De Valera and the Irish cabinet at the Mansion House to discuss the final draft. On his arrival, Michael also gave a copy to Seán Ó Muirthile, one of the top IRB men, who then had a separate meeting with fellow members of the Supreme Council to make their final amendments to the document. Later that evening, having had a harrowing day with De Valera, the cabinet and his fellow delegates, Michael travelled out to Howth, and met with his IRB colleagues. After the meeting, Michael, slipping the document into his brief-case, decided to stay in the area that night. He called in to see the Carmody family, but finding only the two sisters, Nora and Bridget, alone in the house, Michael de-cided it would be prudent not to sleep there – both for security and moral reasons. However, he left the document with the two women for safe-keeping, and taking the cliff path up to Heather Cottage, spent the night with his friend James O'Brien. Early the next morning, Michael called in to Cliff Cottage to collect the precious document, which Nora had kept under her pillow, along with her gun, during the night. He then made his way back to Dublin, catching the boat to England from Dun Laoghaire with Griffith. The other delegates, Barton, Duffy and Childers, had sailed separately from Dublin port.

The Stella Maris convent, at the Bailey, Howth, also had connections with Michael and the rebels. One day in May 1921, three young men called at the con-vent asking for help for one of their wounded comrades. They were all wearing British army uniforms but they quickly told the Sisters that they were Volunteers. Also, one of the men, Joe Leonard, had a sister who was very friendly with the nuns. All three, Emmet Dalton, Joe Leonard and Pat McCrea, were part of Michael's Squad, and had just been involved with a daring daylight attempt to rescue Seán MacEoin, the Blacksmith of Ballinalee, from Mountjoy Jail, where he was awaiting execution. Unfortunately, the attempt failed and one of the men was shot and wounded. However, they all managed to escape in a stolen armoured car, which they later abandoned in Artane, and hiring a taxi, drove out to Howth. Because of Joe's sister's connection, they knew they would be safe at the convent and their wounded comrade taken care of. Seán MacEoin escaped the hangman's rope, and was released shortly after the Truce, in July 1921.

The Volunteers also rented a cottage on the summit of Ben Eadar, although I have no knowledge of its exact location, or if it still exists. Charlie Dalton, younger brother of Emmet, writing in his book *With the Dublin Brigade* mentions having stayed the night at the cottage with Joe Leonard. The following day, a Sunday, the two men walked down to Howth village to attend mass. Later strolling along Main Street, en route to the harbour, they met a newsboy carrying a placard 'Truce to be Arranged Immediately'. This was 26 June 1921; two weeks later it became a reality.

I was told that shortly after the Truce, Michael 'allowed' himself a few days holiday at Heather Cottage to unwind. His friends, especially Joe O'Reilly, often found him wandering around the tracks near the summit, flanked by gorse and bracken high above the blue tranquillity of Dublin Bay, with just the cries of the soaring seagulls to break the silence. He was once found by Joe, lying on his stomach gazing at a flower in total absorption.

I believe Michael's love for Howth continued for the rest of his short life. Whenever he could snatch a few hours away from war and politics, this is where he could be found. However, I would imagine that during the last year of his life, opportunities to get out to Howth, became much harder as his time was taken up with frequent visits to London during the Treaty negotiations, followed by the setting up of the new state and all that it entailed, and then the ensuing Civil War. But it was also during that final year, that Kitty Kiernan was to become the great love of his life, and any spare moments he had, were usually spent in her company. It was to the opposite end of Dublin Bay, in another small fishing village, Greystones, that the lovers went frequently to enjoy the sea air and relative peace and quiet that Michael had once found in Howth. Around 1919 Kitty had, however, with one of her sisters, decided to take a few days holiday in Howth. They stayed at the picturesque Claremont Hotel, overlooking Claremont Strand on the north side of the peninsula, with views across to Ireland's Eye and the Mourne Mountains.

The news of Michael Collins' death reached the village of Howth on Wednesday 23 August 1922, the day after his assassination. A party of Free State soldiers arrived at the St Lawrence Hotel, where a dance was in progress. One made his way across the dance floor and asked the band to stop playing. He then announced the news to the assembled people. The band, without another word, packed up their instruments and left the building. The shocked and grief-stricken crowd also left. That day, the whole village was stunned by the news of Michael's death, the man so many in the community got to know and love over the last eight years

13

MICHAEL REMEMBERED

During the course of my research over the last five years, I have met many interesting people who have helped me to discover the real Michael Collins. Some were direct relations of him or his colleagues. Others were either the children or grandchildren of the various people who knew or worked for him around those tumultuous times. During these meetings, I was told many interesting stories that I feel deserve a chapter to themselves.

Here are a few memories of Michael's only surviving niece, Joan Bunworth who remembered her Uncle Michael when she was a young child growing up on the farm at Woodfield. Joan was born there on 20 December 1916, just a few days before Michael returned to Woodfield for Christmas – having been released from Frongoch camp.

Joan recalls that he would 'often arrive with an entourage' and when Uncle Michael used to visit them, Joan, along with her brothers and sisters would stay outside, keeping a look-out in case any Black and Tans or soldiers appeared. The children always made sure they had a ball or skipping rope with them, so if they had to return to the house quickly to warn their uncle and his friends, they would not arouse suspicion. If ever the soldiers offered them sweets, they always refused, despite sweets being a rare luxury in West Cork during those times. Joan remembered that Uncle Michael had a habit of sitting on, rather than at, the kitchen table, swinging his legs. Her Uncle Michael also charged around the farmyard at Woodfield, revolver in hand, threatening to shoot the ducks and hens. Peig, their housekeeper, stood at the kitchen door shouting to him that she would shoot him first, although she knew he was only fooling around.

Peig was only seventeen when she came to work and look after Johnny Collins' young family on St Patrick's day 1917. His wife Kathleen's health began to fail and she died in February 1921 of TB. In 1922 Johnny remarried, this time to his second cousin Nancy O'Brien. Peig was by then part of the family, and lived with the Collins' for the rest of her life. Many years later, it was revealed that she too had taken many risks and played her part in West Cork's fight for independence from Britain.

Joan also remembered her father Johnny Collins, telling her about an incident with Uncle Michael, which took place when he was around nine years old. Johnny and Michael were walking along a laneway near Woodfield when an old woman passed them by, carrying a heavy load of turf on her back. She was walking very slowly, bent double with the weight. Michael suddenly clambering up onto the stone-wall, shouted to the old lady: 'When I'm a man, women will never have to carry turf on their backs again'.

As a young child of four, Joan experienced the trauma of being present when the Essex Regiment, under a Major Percival, arrived to burn Woodfield on 7 April 1921, as a reprisal for a recent attack on the RIC barracks at Rosscarbery. When the soldiers stormed into the house, Joan remembered her little brother Liam, who was only a few months old at the time, being snatched out of his cradle. She also vividly remembered watching one of the soldiers pushing his bayonet behind a large wall clock, which when prized free, crashed down onto the stone floor in front of her. With the soldiers were several neighbours, who, at bayonet point, were forced to bring hay and straw into the house and then ignite it with petrol. The house, including all the family heirlooms and the children's schoolbooks, was destroyed by fire. One outbuilding, which was being used as a stable, and happened to be part of the original house that Michael had been born in, survived.

Another of the Collins' family loaned me a recording of Joan's younger stepbrother Michael (later of Waterford) who, in emotional tones, recalled his father Johnny's account of the more unpleasant realities of that night and its aftermath. The soldiers had arrived with a mixture of Black and Tans and the farm, which had been in the family for 250 years, was burnt within fifteen minutes. Watching the destruction of her home and clutching a new school satchel, a recent present from her father, was Michael's terrified step-sister Kitty. At one point Percival himself grabbed the satchel out of her hand and threw it into the flames saying, 'that won't go to school with you'.

At the same time, two of Kitty's sisters and her brother Pat, were ordered at bayonet point to round up all the hens, geese, ducks, chickens, turkeys and guinea fowl, 368 in all, and drive them into one of the outhouses where they were subsequently destroyed.

One of the soldiers said at the time how he hated having to be involved with such an awful business, thinking of his own wife and family in England, but if he did not obey orders, he too would have been shot. Another soldier managed to save the family sewing machine whilst Percival's back was turned. As Woodfield smouldered, Percival and his soldiers clambered back into their armoured cars and drove off into the night, to burn three further houses in the neighbourhood.

Johnny Collins was arrested as he got off the Cork train at Clonakilty Station, at the same time as Woodfield was being torched. He was held at Spike Island prison, just outside of Cork city, and not released until shortly before Christmas 1921. After the burning of Woodfield, the family were scattered. Peig looked after the two youngest children in an outhouse of a relative Annie Collins, who lived next door to the now ruined farm. Neighbouring families took in the other children, but at great risk to themselves as they too could have been visited by British soldiers and suffered the same fate. The family were finally reunited when Johnny married Nancy O'Brien in 1922.

Despite all that had happened, Michael's father, Johnny, always said, 'Don't let any of my children be bitter. Bitterness is self-destructive. It only destroys the man or woman who is bitter'.

Michael Collins on hearing of the destruction of Woodfield, summed up his personal feelings – 'they knew how to hurt me!'

Nancy O'Brien also had some amusing stories about Michael. At the height of the 'Tan' war, Nancy was in lodgings in Iona Road, Glasnevin, Dublin, a few doors down from a friend of hers, a Mrs Murphy, a widow, and her family. Nancy also lodged with them for a while. Occasionally, her cousin Michael used the Murphy's residence as a safe-house. Each morning Polly, one of the daughters, gave Michael his 'early' breakfast. This, he ate heartily but never thought to thank Polly. Instead, he would bound back up the stairs into Mrs Murphy's bedroom, whilst she was enjoying her morning cup of tea, and with a quick kiss and hug, would thank her for her kindness and hospitality.

Around the same time 1920-21, Michael was visiting a friend who was ill at the Mater Hospital in Dublin. Suddenly there was a raid by the Auxiliaries. Michael, realising the danger, slipped into one of the private rooms in which lay an ailing bishop. Diving under the bed, he hid there until the raid was over. Fortunately, the poor bishop was too ill to notice his famous intruder.

Michael could be quite indifferent about using people, even his own family, as couriers! Around 1920, when Nancy was working at the Harmon Buildings, at that time was part of the GPO, her father was taken seriously ill. As she arranged to go back to Cork to see him, one of Michael's men, calling himself Danny Navan, (not his real name) came over to her at work and insisted on handing over a hold-all, together with 'instructions' from Michael. She was to take it with her on the train down to Cork and make her way to a certain convent in the city, where she would receive further directions. Nancy was also advised to be careful during her journey down, and not to let anyone else handle the hold-all, which was extremely heavy. She quickly realised that it contained guns and ammunition for the West Cork flying columns. Unfortunately, just before the train arrived at Cork city, British troops boarded the train and began searching the passengers. Nancy, already upset about her father and worried about the illegal cargo she was carrying, burst into tears. Fortunately, the soldiers took pity on her and left her alone – one even offered to carry the heavy hold-all! On her arrival at the convent, she received further instructions to hand over the bag, with its illicit cargo, to one of the 'nuns'. With her task accomplished, Nancy, heaving a sigh of relief, went on to visit her sickly father. On her return to Dublin, she informed Michael that the mission had been a success but her arms, during the process, had grown a few inches longer!

Maureen Kirwin, Michael's grand-niece, related a couple of family memories to me. One day when Michael was about eight, his brothers went out working in the fields and his mother and sisters, except for his older sister Mary, took the day off to visit a local fair. Noticing how busy she was, little Michael decided to help her with preparing the evening meal by going out into the garden and digging up some potatoes. Some time later he staggered back into the kitchen, dragging a bucketful of potatoes, and saying, 'I have them nearly all dug!' Later that evening, his older brother thanked him for his hard work and Michael asked Johnny could he have three-pence? 'Of course you can,' said Johnny, 'but what for?

Michael said he been reading lately the works of a man called Arthur Griffith, the founder of a new political party Sinn Féin – Ourselves Alone – and he wanted to buy his weekly pamphlet *Scissors & Paste* to learn more about Griffith's ideas. Twenty-four years later, shortly before he died, Griffith's said: 'I have no ambition that my name go down in Irish history, but if it does, I want it to be associated with the name of Michael Collins'.

Another incident was when Michael was on the run, and staying with the O'Connor family in Brendan Road. Early one morning, the Auxiliaries raided the house and Michael, unusually, was still asleep in bed. The O'Connor's maid, realising the danger Michael was in, quickly rushed upstairs and grabbing a spare mattress, threw it on top of the still sleeping Michael. She then began to beat it vigorously, pretending to be busy with spring-cleaning, whilst the soldiers searched the house. After they had gone, unable to find their quarry, a somewhat shaken but very grateful Michael, emerged from between the mattresses.

Fionnuala Donovan's grandmother, Julia, lived with her family at 16 Airfield Road, one of Michael's two main safe houses in Dublin. Fionnuala related some interesting stories about her family and those times. All of Julia's children were sworn to secrecy about their visiting 'uncles' Mick and Gearóid (O'Sullivan) from West Cork. One day Sheila, who was about eighteen at the time, was walking down O'Connell Street, or Sackville Street as it was then known, when Michael breezed past her on his bicycle, and pulled up to say hello. She walked on, totally ignoring him, having been warned by Michael himself, never to acknowledge or speak to him outside of their home. It was also around the time he had a ransom of £10,000 on his head. Back at Airfield Road, he jibbed 'Why Miss High and Mighty couldn't pass the time of day with him'.

But she quickly retorted, 'It was he who had instructed her never to do so in public!'

Julia, a widow, had one maid who did not realise who the two 'uncles' really were, although she unwittingly referred to Gearóid as the 'Little Fellow' and Michael as the 'Big Fellow'. Julia ran three dairies in the south Dublin area, and she allowed the 'boys' to make full use of her business, smuggling pistols in the butter boxes and rifles in the egg cases. Also, as a safety precaution, Julia had a small hole cut in one of the glass side panels of the front door at 16 Airfield Road, so that anyone inside could see who was at the door before opening it.

Michael always got on very well with Julia's fatherless children, playing with the smaller ones and helping the older ones with their homework or problems. He often quoted from the famous 'Sixth Book', the classic and comprehensive reader that he and Julia had both used when they were children at school. He was also

Photograph taken outside No. 16 Airfield Road, Rathgar, Dublin on 22 November 1920
Back row: *Julia O'Donovan (bride's aunt), Michael Collins, Gearóid O'Sullivan, Mrs P. O'Keeffe (wife of Cork TD, Paudeen O'Keeffe), Seán Hyde (vet and member of Michael's ASU), Denis and Alice Lynch and Jim Murray*
Middle row: *Fr Bonaventure, OFM, Sheila O'Donovan (bridesmaid), Elizabeth Clancy (bride), Michael J. O'Brien (groom), Mick Lynch (best man), Joe Clancy (brother of the bride) and Pat Barry (uncle of the bride)*
Front row: *Ted Clancy (nee O'Donovan, Joe's wife), Eileen O'Donovan, Seán O'Donovan, Dona O'Donovan and Tadhg O'Donovan*

very friendly with the Ryan family a few doors down the road and often played football with the boys. Occasionally, in an emergency, he used their loft as a hiding place, which, being full of hay was always quite comfortable and warm.

An Anglo-Irish Protestant family lived close to Julia in Airfield Road. They could have easily informed the authorities of all the suspicious comings and goings at No. 16. However, Julia had come to the family's aid one night, helping to deliver a baby that arrived prematurely and the family were extremely grateful to her. Even if they had had any suspicions about the various visitors to No. 16, they kept quiet about Michael, Gearóid or other frequent guests arriving at the house at all times of the day or night.

Around July of 1922, Julia and her family were to move a few streets away to a much larger house in Garville Avenue. Michael, despite his busy schedule was very eager to see the new house and how the family were settling in. He even managed to have dinner with them a couple of times before his final visit to Cork in August. A few weeks after his death, Julia invited some of his old friends around for tea including Gearóid O'Sullivan and Kevin O'Higgins. As they were gathered in the dining-room, word came that the 'Irregulars' (anti-Treatyites) were about to raid the place and possibly arrest the men inside. They immediately scrambled out of the window and hid in the garden, leaving Julia's children to eat up all the goodies left on the table! As things turned out, it was a false alarm.

I had an interesting discussion with a Michael Collins of Castlefreke, a village a couple of miles south from Woodfield, near the coast. His father Jim, was born in 1888, and was Michael's first cousin. The two cousins, being of similar ages, grew up together, and as lads used to catch eels and fish in the Owenahincha, the stream that flowed below the farm at Woodfield. During the summer months the boys loved to visit the beach at Owenahincha where their aunt, Mrs Kate O'Brien, had a small cottage. This was one of the three beaches in close proximity to Woodfield where Michael's own family would often go. Around 1903, the night that Michael's (Castlefreke) grandfather died, Jim and Michael went to collect the 'winding sheet' from a relative. On their return to Castlefreke that night, the two boys said they could hear the banshee (a female ghost that wails) haunting them on their journey back. After the funeral, Michael and Jim had an argument as to whether Robert Emmet was really a hero of the 1798 Rebellion. Michael, as usual, thought he had the correct answer, although he was only thirteen at the time.

After Michael went to London in 1906, Jim stayed on at the family farm. He became interested in the Sinn Féin movement around 1916 and went to his first meeting with Johnny Collins, Michael's older brother, at Dunmanway in January 1917. Johnny was chairman at the time. Jim later became involved with the IRA and the Volunteers and, during the War of Independence, rose to the rank of captain in the local Rosscarbery flying column. He also joined the Gaelic League mainly because of his interest in step-dancing which, as a young boy, he had learned from a 'hedge' school dance master. Step-dancing, a very old form of Irish dancing, was frowned upon by the English educational authorities, who at the time ran all the local National Schools.

Michael of Castlefreke also recalled his father's memories of Christmas 1916. Michael, having been released from Frongoch on 22 December 1916, returned to Ireland. Having stopped off in Dublin for a couple of days, to see some old friends and enjoy a 'few' pints, he travelled down by train to West Cork on Christmas day – still the worse for wear. The train only went as far as Clonakilty, and as none of his family were able to meet him at the station, Michael had to walk the last couple of miles to Woodfield on a bitterly cold night, only to find his maternal grandmother had just died.

He was full of enthusiasm to continue the fight against England for Ireland's freedom, and this did not go down too well with some of the older members of the family, or indeed the local parish priest, Father Hill. He had baptised both Michael and his cousin Jim, and seen them grow from babies to becoming alter boys at his new parish church at nearby Lisavaird. At mass the following Sunday, knowing that Michael was amongst his congregation, Father Hill decided to give a strong anti-Sinn Féin, anti-Volunteer sermon. After mass, an incensed Michael, returning along the lane to Woodfield, joined in a game of bowls with some local lads. Suddenly, he scrambled up onto the hedge, and facing his audience, bellowed down at them, 'I'd rather be in hell with Tomás Mac Donagh, than go to heaven with that man!'

Bowling had always been a favourite pastime of Michael's since he was a small boy and whenever he was back home in Woodfield for a holiday, he would enjoy a game with his friends and relations. It was, and still is, played mainly in West Cork and Co. Armagh, although the way it is played varies slightly between the two counties. West Cork men swing their arms before throwing the ball and the idea of the game is to go from A to B with the least number of bowls. Michael (of Castlefreke) told me that many years ago a small cannon ball was sometimes used. The earliest known photograph of Michael also has a bowling connection (see p. 8). It was taken when he was about eleven, wearing a smart suit and cap, standing with his mother, grandmother, sister and brother Johnny, outside their new house in Woodfield. Michael had just been given a penny and was anxious to join his friends in a game of bowls down the lane. However, his mother told him to stay, as she wanted him in the photograph as well, hence a scowl. The traditional game of bowling was not so popular in cities, although I heard, to compensate, Michael also enjoyed handball, a game similar to tennis but using the bare palm of the hand instead of a racket, to hit the ball. He would occasionally indulge in a game with his friends and colleagues in Dublin.

Joan Browne heard some interesting anecdotes from her grandmother, Mary Butterley. Although Mary was born and reared in the Howth area, she frequently went down to West Cork, accompanied by her mother Bridget, spending their summer holidays at Woodfield, with the Collins family. The two cousins, Michael and Mary, with only four years difference between them, were good friends. As children, they often played together in the hay-ricks or went fishing, taking a small boat out onto the Owenahincha stream, which flowed between the fields, below Woodfield. Mary, who was a good swimmer, used to tease Michael because he could not swim, and had no desire to learn. He hated the thought of being immersed in water, although this aversion did not stop him years later, pushing his colleagues overboard into the river Tolka.

After Michael returned to Dublin in 1916, he renewed his friendship with Mary and they continued to spend time together. They often cycled across the old wooden bridge and along Bull Wall, part of Bull Island near Clontarf, close to where another aunt, Mrs O'Brien Twohig, lived at 'Craigmillar', Haddon Road. They both enjoyed walking along the local beaches and especially the beach at Sutton, which they accessed through what was then known as the 'hole in the wall' possibly Lauders Lane, between Sutton Cross and station. This led to the sand dunes and beautiful unspoilt stretch of beach, between Sutton and Howth, a distance of two miles. Today, Sutton golf course and club house covers part of that area. Joan also remembered her grandmother saying what a generous person Michael was, and how he enjoyed giving people presents. He once gave her a Faberge broach as a birthday gift.

Mary later married a Dublinman, John Joseph Boland who worked for Paramount Films. They had eight children, and Róisín, became an Abbey Theatre actress. The couple first went to live in Ferguson Road, Glasnevin and later bought Beverley Hall on the Howth Road, near Killester, fairly close to Moya Llewelyn Davies' house Furry Park. Whether the two women ever met is not known, but with Michael's social connections, it is quite possible.

Joan also said that Michael used his relations scattered around Dublin to help him in various ways. I have already mentioned his use of the Butterley home in Howth during the *Asgard* gun-running. He also used his aunt Mrs O'Brien Twohig's house in Clontarf as a safe-house. Michael had a complete network of family and friends that helped him both financially, as well as providing offices or safe houses. Mary's husband, John Boland, had an uncle who rented an office at No. 32 Bachelors Walk and this was one of Michael's main offices during the War of Independence.

Bridget Butterley, Mary's mother, had two sisters, Minnie Dearham and Nell Keating, both living in the Dublin area. These two aunts were also very helpful to Michael, letting him use their homes as safe-houses, as well as supporting him financially in various fund-raising schemes.

A further interesting insight into Michael and how his family background helped him to develop into the man he was came out after chatting to Joan Browne and later to Peg O'Driscoll (*nee* O'Brien). On both Michael's father's and mother's sides, the families were prosperous and well educated. Obviously, this reflected onto Michael, not only his interests in literature, theatre and the arts, but also the way he dressed – always very dapper and well turned out. Even at the GPO in 1916, Michael, resplendent in his staff captain's uniform, was one of the few Volunteers who could afford to look the part. He had natural good taste, and throughout his life, from childhood and his early days in London with his sister, always enjoyed a reasonably good standard of living. Even during the War of Independence, most of his safe-houses, Furry Park being no exception, were in the main, quite comfortable quarters for a man on the run. Michael also possessed an in-bred self-esteem, coupled with natural social skills, which certainly helped him cope with the many challenges he had to face during his life.

Michael White of Sams Cross,told me that during the War of Independence, his father, David, became a Sinn Féin judge, at the Sinn Féin Courts, which were held in defiance to the British ones. He also helped Michael collect funds for the National Loan in 1919, around the Clonakilty area. In June 1922, Michael Collins was touring around his constituency in West Cork, 'flogging' the Treaty, just before

Michael Collins with a group in Killarney after a Pro-Treaty rally, 22 April 1922

the Pact Election. Michael White, then a young schoolboy, remembered seeing him for the last time when Michael Collins visited Lisavaird School to meet his former schoolmaster, Denis Lyons. Little Michael was in the classroom at the time, eating his lunch, when suddenly in walked his father, along with Michael Collins, who introduced him to his son saying, 'Mick, this is another Michael'. Later that day, Michael Collins called to see another old friend, James Santry at the forge in Lisavaird, for a chat, and afterwards treated him to a pint at the pub next door.

Michael White also remembered Michael Collins' convoy passing through Sams Cross, on its way to Woodfield. The local people along with their children, were all out working in the fields, threshing the corn, on that warm, still, fateful day in August 1922. A few hours later, they were to hear the dreadful news that 'Mickeen was no more'.

Peg O'Driscoll remembered her father (Jim O'Brien) saying that as youngster he and his brother often played football with Michael Collins and some other local lads, in a field behind the farm at Woodfield. Michael was a very good player but even then he always had to win, and took any form of defeat very badly. After any match, if Michael disagreed with the score, his side having lost, he would storm off across the fields, raging.

Michael spent his last Christmas back at Sam's Cross, visiting his family and friends. On the morning of Christmas Day, 1921, accompanied by his older brother Johnny, he ascended the great whale-back hill of Knockfeen, or Carraig-a-Radhairc as it is known locally, overlooking Woodfield. Taking in its panoramic views up to the distant peaks of the Kerry mountains to the north and down to the scattered farms and villages, nestling along the rugged coastline of Rosscarbery Bay to the south, Michael quietly remarked to his brother, 'I've seen more of my own country this morning, than I have ever seen in my whole life'.

The same Christmas, when Peg's father asked Michael about the rumours of a romantic nature, linking him with certain society ladies, including Hazel Lavery during the Treaty talks in London, Michael's reply was that during those months in London, they rarely had time to get a proper nights sleep, let along time for romances.

Around 1943, Peg, as a young woman, came up to Dublin from West Cork to work. Peg soon got to know Michael's older brother, Johnny, and his second wife Nancy O'Brien. Sometimes, over a bank holiday, the Collins' would invite her to stay with them at their home in Booterstown, a pleasant residential area just a couple of miles south of the city, along Dublin Bay. Johnny and Nancy always went to the 7 a.m. mass at the local church, as did De Valera and his wife Sinead, who were also living in Booterstown. After the service Johnny and De Valera, accompanied by their wives, chatting together arm in arm, would walk part of the way home together. Despite their differences in politics, the two men had a great respect for one another, going back to their early days and the fight for Irish freedom.

Peg, remembered Nancy talking about Michael: 'He was a big-hearted man but would fly into a rage if everything wasn't just right. However, he never forgot that my favourite sweets were either marshmallows or bulls-eyes, and often bought me a bag, to make amends.' Nancy also confessed that she was more than a little fond of her second cousin Michael, and despite his bad moods and tempers, she had grown to love him over the years.

When talking one day to Máire Cruise O'Brien, a fellow resident of Howth, she told me about her mother, Margaret Browne and Michael Collins. Before Margaret married Seán MacEntee, she was very involved in helping Michael throughout the War of Independence. She first met him at a Prisoners Aid Rally around 1919 and fell completely under his spell. Her work for him mainly involved carrying dispatches and messages around Dublin, and being a woman, Margaret was rarely stopped or searched by the authorities. Occasionally, Michael also used her flat in Parnell Square, above what was then Leinster College, as a safe-house. Sadly, this friendship ceased after the signing of the Treaty in December 1921, when Margaret and her husband Seán, both took the anti-Treaty side.

Lian Breslin, from Ferns, Co. Wexford, related another rather amusing story to me. Her grandmother was another of Michael's couriers, who enlisted the aid of Lian's father – a small baby at the time. Vital messages, to and from Michael, were tucked safely inside the baby's nappy! While baby and mother would regularly pass soldiers or Auxiliaries, they in turn would never dream of searching a young woman with her child. Their only comment, if they happened to stop and look into the pram was – 'Ah musha, what a cute little baby you have there!'

Frank and Peadar Lawlor still live in the Arbour Hill district of Dublin. Their father Laurence, along with his brother Frank, joined the Volunteers in 1913, and was part of 'A' Company First Battalion in Dublin. They were both involved with the Rising of 1916, fighting around the Four Courts and North King Street area. They also joined Sinn Féin and the Gaelic League, attending meetings and ceilidhes at the Colm Cille hall in Blackhall Street. However, it was through their secret membership of the IRB that they first met Michael in Dublin. The three men met again when they were all interned in Frongoch. Peadar explained how Michael, immediately after he had been taken prisoner in 1916 and interned at Richmond Barracks, began to gather names and addresses of men who would help him fight the next round against the British. He continued doing this whilst he was at Stafford Goal and later in Frongoch. Around 1917, when all the prisoners were finally released, the *Irish Times* printed a list of the names and addresses of all the men who had been involved in the Rising and during the War of Independence – the Black and Tans were to find this very useful!

Frank Lawlor recalled his father's memories of his time spent at Frongoch camp in Wales. The wooden huts were only a few feet apart and with the volume of men tramping about, the ground between the huts became very muddy, even in June, when they first arrived, and even worse during the winter months. During those early days of winter in late 1916 when the snow began to fall, the men were allowed to make toboggans. The younger men in their twenties, including Michael, enjoyed a bit of horseplay. The toboggans were designed to take about six men, but twice this number would often pile aboard, which was quite dangerous and could have easily resulted in a serious accident or even death. However, the only comment at the time from the captain in charge of the camp was 'The more that they kill themselves, the less mouths for us to feed'.

After the brother's were released, around Christmas 1916, Laurence, a carpenter by trade, decided not to return to the place where he was working as it was owned by an Englishman called Keating. Instead, he found a position with an Irish company called Saunders, near to St Stephen's Green. Both men went back to their old battalion and continued to work for Michael throughout the Tan war. Along with the rest of the family, they were involved with helping Michael to collect funds for the Dáil Loan, especially gold sovereigns, which could be paid straight into Irish banks. They knew a fellow IRB man called MacCullagh, who at the time, worked for a piano and musical instrument specialist, Pigotts, in Suffolk Street. The brothers arranged with MacCullagh to have some of the money hidden in a coffin. It was then buried under the cobblestones, below the archway leading to the yard behind Pigotts. Only Michael and the IRB men knew the exact whereabouts of the hidden money.

During the Tan War, their cousin, Liam Mongey, from Castlebar, Co. Mayo, came up to Dublin as a medical student. Liam was also a Volunteer and it was he, who devised hook attachments for grenades. This lethal adaptation became very effective when hurling them at passing 'caged' Tan troop lorries, as the grenades became difficult to unhook from the vehicles before exploding with devastating results.

Peadar also told me a couple of amusing stories that his father had recalled about Michael during the 'Tan' war. Michael was staying at the Gresham Hotel one evening, when he heard it was about to be raided by the Black and Tans. Thinking quickly how he was to escape without being noticed, he remembered the woman in the room next to his was quite friendly. Knocking on her door, he asked if he could briefly borrow her coat, hat, handbag and umbrella, and although she was somewhat perplexed, she let him go ahead. Fortunately the woman was fairly tall and well built, so Michael had no problem fitting into her coat, which I assume was a long one, to cover his trousers and boots. He then went downstairs and walked out of the hotel's main entrance. On seeing a British officer waiting for someone by the hotel door, Michael, in his best 'English, female' voice asked the officer 'Could you call me a cab please!' Fortunately, one arrived immediately and Michael, climbing in, disappeared into the night, his quick thinking, yet again, saving his life.

Peadar told me a story me about Michael and Conor Clune, who was murdered, along with Dick McKee and Peadar Clancy, by the Auxiliaries in November 1921. Conor had come up from the country and was staying at the Exchange Hotel, in Exchequer Street, another of Michael's haunts. The porter, who was also a spy for the British, became suspicious of Conor, as he had no luggage with him, and immediately informed one of the detectives at the Castle. Later that evening, he made his way over to Vaughans Hotel, to join Michael and some of his men for a meeting, but had not realised that he had been followed by a 'G' man. Fortunately, someone, possibly Dave Neligan, rang Michael and warned him that Vaughans was about to be raided. Michael was out of the hotel and half way down the street by the time the Black and Tans arrived. Conor escaped over the back wall of the hotel and into the next garden. Unfortunately, as he climbed over the garden wall into Granby Lane, a soldier accosted him and asked him where he was going and why was he out so late – it was well after the curfew. Conor said he had been playing cards with his friends and forgotten the time. Luckily the soldier was sympathetic and sent Conor on his way, with a 'Go on now or else you'll get no sleep tonight!'

At the commencement of the Civil War in June 1922, Frank and Peadar's father Laurence, took the Republican side, supporting De Valera, while their uncle Frank, took Michael's side and joined the new Free State army. However, to both men Michael was always the 'Big Fellow'.

A couple of miles north of Dublin city centre, along the bay near Clontarf, just off the Malahide Road, stands a fascinating and now beautifully restored folly known as Marino Casino. Built in the mid eighteenth century for a Lord Charlemont as a private casino, card games and gambling being popular amongst the wealthy at the time, it stood in the grounds of his now long vanished country residence. The building was connected to the house by a tunnel, used originally to convey people during inclement weather. The tunnel, which survives, also has an in-

Passageway originally built leading to Charlemont house, under Marino Casino, Clontarf and used to practice and store Thompson sub-machine guns in 1921

Later version of Thompson sub-machine gun

teresting connection with Michael Collins, something I discovered when talking to the local guide.

Around early 1921, at the height of the War of Independence, the IRB through its' American connections with Clan na Gael, helped finance and develop in America, a still secret weapon known as the Thompson sub-machine gun. Back in Ireland, very few people except Michael and his close associates in the IRB even knew of the existence of this most deadly of weapons. In the spring of 1921, Clan na Gael arranged for a few of these sub machine guns to be smuggled into Dublin port, by two ex-Irish-American army officers, who would give Michael and his men a demonstration on how to assemble, load and fire the guns. However, the problem then was finding somewhere discreet and convenient for the Volunteers to be trained in the handling of these new guns, the noise from which, when fired, was deafening. Fortunately, the Christian Brothers, who ran an orphanage in Clontarf, were also very sympathetic to the Volunteers, allowing them to use their grounds for drilling purposes. Close to the orphanage, surrounded by open spaces was the old Marino Casino folly, with its disused underground tunnel. This was brick lined, wide, dry, and naturally illuminated by periodic pools of light coming from the air vents in its roof, making it an ideal venue. Michael, along with Harry Boland, Tom Barry and Gearóid O'Sullivan, together with members of the Dublin Active Service Unit had the perfect location for their deafening practice sessions. The gun, which had amazing fire-power, was also easy to dismantle and conceal. This impressed both Michael and his men, and he immediately ordered a further 500 to be purchased in America and shipped over to Ireland. Just before the ship, with its illegal cargo, sailed from America, the US customs department raided it – the result of a tip off from British intelligence – and not only the guns but also a large sum of money was lost.

Marino Casino

Minister for Justice, Kevin O'Higgins, and Col Joe O'Reilly with Mrs Danny O'Brien, Michael's aunt, and her grand-daughters – Mary (O'Brien) Hodnett and Peg (O'Brien) O'Driscoll – at Sam's Cross, Clonakilty

14

MICHAEL COLLINS AND HIS RELEVANCE TODAY

If ever I am asked about Michael Collins' relevance in today's Ireland, my reply is that he was the one person who laid down the foundations of the Ireland we all now enjoy. Had he lived, it is very likely that Ireland would have become one of Europe's most prosperous and wealthy nations fifty years earlier, as she finally now is, at beginning of the twenty-first century. Because of his premature death, not only Ireland's prosperity but also the tragedy and bitterness of the Civil War and of the north, with its years of conflict, which sadly continues to this day, would most likely have been averted.

His vision in setting up the new Free State would be, in many ways, as applicable today, as it was eighty years ago. He was responsible for inaugurating the new civic guard, or the garda siochána as it is now called, and for creating the new Free State peace-keeping army. As Minister for Finance, he set in place many of the financial initiatives that underpinned the new state and these continue to be used to this day in the present Department of Finance. He was also the brains behind setting up the independent New Ireland Assurance Company, later to be one of Ireland's largest insurance companies.

During February 1922, on a tour in Dungarvan, Michael was approached by an American senator who asked him: 'Mr Collins, now that you've secured the military freedom of your country, how can you possibly survive economically?' Michael's reply was even more relevant now than it was eighty years ago. 'We will survive economically if we export to the growing sophisticated markets of the world, goods of quality which they're entitled to demand at a price beyond which they will not pay and on the day they rightly demand delivery. To meet this there is only one criteria, the pursuit of excellence.' Today, Ireland is doing just this, exporting to the sophisticated markets of the world.

Six weeks before his death, at the outbreak of the Civil War, Michael wrote to Desmond Fitzgerald, then Minister for Propaganda, suggesting films be made and shown around the country's numerous cinemas. The first, a 'war film', was to promote the new National Army as the Irish peoples' army, and to demonstrate to the 'plain' people of Ireland, that its fight against the anti-Treatyites was for the peace and prosperity of the newly created Free State.

The second film was to be 'educational' and portrayed Michael's vision of how Ireland's trade and industries could be rebuilt and revitalised after the recent War of Independence and the now on-going Civil War. He began, by pointing out the enormous value of Ireland's fishing industry and how it should now invest in well-equipped, up-to-date trawlers. That was followed by the idea of setting up a forestry department to plant pines and other trees on the bare mountains of Ireland and to revive the Irish timber industry. Coupled with that, were plans for a proper drainage system and the reclaiming of flooded land across the country. The use of hydro-electric and peat burning power stations to generate cheap electricity was another of his visions for the future. To use Michael's own words: 'As in Italy, nearly every little village there has its electric engine to operate light, heat and power.' Within a decade, the Shannon Scheme was to do just that. He also wanted to deal with the dreadful housing conditions prevalent at the time in both towns and cities, with the film featuring slum clearances and the building of new garden suburbs.

Michael wanted to encourage foreign investment into Ireland, as well as state intervention, to help expand and export Irish products to the world – cheese and dairy products, brewing and distilling industry, along with tobacco manufacturing. Ireland's woollen, linen and clothing factories were also to be encouraged to expand production and export more of their unique Irish products to the markets of Britain and Europe. On Ireland's cultural side, art, music, plays, literature and language were to be supported, but not controlled, by central government, and promoted not only throughout Ireland but also abroad.

Now, eighty years on, most of Michael's ideas have come to fruition. Ireland is famous the world over for her food products, her unique clothing and fashion industry and her numerous musical and cultural contributions, *Riverdance* possibly being the most celebrated. Guinness, Baileys and Jameson whiskey, is drunk and enjoyed around the four corners of the globe. Today, Ireland not only culturally and industrially, but also politically has her place in both the European and the world's arena. I am sure Michael would have been amazed and delighted that what he had hoped for his country's future has in many ways finally happened. Even the tensions in the north have, since the Good Friday Agreement, eased, with a cease-fire and the co-operation of the various political parties. Hopefully the two factions will one day live together in peace and harmony, and perhaps Ireland will indeed become 'A Nation Once Again' – Michael's ultimate dream.

When he died a couple of months before his thirty-second birthday, his skills as a statesman were still developing and none could have dreamed of what he may have accomplished had he lived. Michael was a great thinker and in his new role as chairman of the new Free State in early 1922, he realised that countries like Germany, Denmark and Holland enjoyed a more up-to-date system of government than Ireland. One of his first tasks was to contact the government departments of each country, to ask their advice as to how he could apply some of their progressive ideas to the setting up and governing the new Free State. He played to win and had the vision, tenacity and sheer ruthlessness to have created the Ireland he had dreamed about. He had, throughout his life, the strength to stand up for what he believed in, whether it was against Britain, or later, as the Civil War clouds darkened across Ireland, against his own former colleagues.

Woodfield, Michael's birthplace

Although, throughout most of the twentieth century, Michael was airbrushed out of history, he was never forgotten. His brothers, sisters, nephews and nieces, remembered him with pride and sadness. Also, his old friends and comrades were never to forget what the 'Big Fellow' had done for them and their country.

With the passing of the generations Michael was restored to his rightful place in Irish history. In August 1965, at Sams Cross, West Cork, just half a mile away from his birthplace, a huge boulder mounted with a bronze plaque bearing Michael's profile, was unveiled. At the ceremony, along with Michael Collins' nephew was General Tom Barry, a close colleague of Michael's during the War of Independence but later to take the anti-Treaty side. Despite this difference of opinion, Barry's ad-

Statue of Michael in Emmet Square, Clonakilty – unveiled by Liam Neeson, 22 August 2002

dress at the unveiling was to sum Michael up thus: 'No man, inside Ireland or outside it, contributed more than Michael Collins to the fight for Irish Independence'.

1990 was to see another milestone in reinstating Michael's image into the forefront of Irish history – the restoration of Woodfield, the family home burned down in April 1921 by the Essex Regiment. The site lay derelict for many years, much of the stone being used by local farmers and what buildings had survived, also fell into disrepair. In 1986, the then owners of Woodfield, Denis and Catherine Coakley, decided to hand back the homestead to Liam Collins, Michael's nephew. Liam then undertook the task of restoring not only Michael's but also his own birthplace, clearing scrub and undergrowth, and laying down lawns and pathways. Only the foundations of the house built in 1900 survived but the building that Michael was born in, later used as a cowshed, was lovingly restored. Perhaps the most striking memorial at Woodfield is the beautiful bronze bust of Michael by Francis Doyle Jones, mounted on a plinth. It was presented by the family of Joe McGrath, one of his closest friends and fellow member of the IRB. I was told that it was actually cast while Michael was alive but for many years lay gathering dust in the cellars of the National Museum in Dublin.

The Michael Collins Memorial Centre, as it is now known, was officially opened on 14 October 1990 just two days before the centenary of Michael's birth. The ceremony included members from all religious and political persuasions, together with many of the Collins family, in the company of friends and relations of people associated with him. Dr Patrick Hillery, then Ireland's president, gave the inauguration speech, and Liam Collins gave the closing speech, on what was to be one of West Cork's wettest days for a long time!

But today it is the annual commemorations at Glasnevin and Beál na mBláth that are the most poignant reminders of his tragic death – not only for his family but also for his many friends and admirers. Every year, usually the third Sunday in August, a Requiem Mass is held in memory of both Michael and Arthur Griffith at St Joseph's Church in Berkeley Road, Phibsborough, Dublin. Once only at-

The limestone cross at Beál na mBláth

tended by the Collins or Griffith family and a few close friends, it is now the child-ren or grand-children of Michael's and Arthur's families and friends, who have taken their place, proud in the knowledge that their parents or grandparents had been related, or had known, two such great men. Following the service, the congre-gation proceeds up to Glasnevin cemetery, less than a mile away, to lay wreaths on the graves of the two old friends, who were to die within ten days of each other.

Beál na mBláth or 'The Mouth of the Flowers' is a section of the lonely 'B' road from Dunmanway to Crookstown, which meanders through the beautiful rolling countryside of West Cork and is the setting for the other annual commemoration.

Due to felled trees and blown bridges, Michael and his touring party had to take the circuitous route from Bandon back to Cork city. It was here, as the evening closed in and a light drizzle began to fall, that the convoy drove into an IRA ambush and Michael, countermanding Dalton's orders to drive on, shouted: 'Stop, and we'll fight them!' The rest is history and other than to say that Michael was the only person in the convoy to be killed, the circumstances surrounding the ambush

Michael's grave in Glasnevin

and who pulled the trigger, I will leave to the historians and experts.

The ceremony to commemorate Michael's death has been held here every year since 1923, normally on the Sunday closest to 22 August. Over the past years, despite the fact that those who would have personally known Michael and had lived through those times, have nearly all died, as with Glasnevin, the children and grandchildren of those people now attend in their hundreds. At the first anniversary of Michael's death, a plain wooden cross was unveiled, close to the spot where he died. The following year, 1924, a beautiful limestone cross was erected, bearing the crucified Christ. Only Michael's name and the date of his death, in Irish, are engraved at the base. The cross was erected on a stone platform, surrounded by iron railings and with steps to gain access.

Michael's family, friends and the new Free State army, attended the first two memorial services in 1923 and 1924. However, the army's presence, except for the fiftieth anniversary in 1972, when the road was widened to take the extra crowds and traffic, was disallowed from 1932 after Fianna Fáil came into power. Its' absence was to continue for a number of years until Ireland's Civil War politics and the generation who lived through it, finally faded away.

As Michael died without making a will, a Grant of Administration Intestate was issued on 21 September 1922, leaving the sum of £1,950.9s.11d. Johnny Collins, Michael's oldest brother who was then living at 89 Botanic Road, Glasnevin, administered this, paying Michael's funeral expenses of £109.18s.6d., as well as other outstanding debts totalling £24.16s.11d. This included unpaid bills to both the Gresham and Hibernia Hotels, and T. J. Callaghan & Co. Military Tailors of Dame Street, Dublin, amongst others. What remained after all Michael's debts were paid was shared amongst his siblings. The document states that Michael was Commander-in-Chief of the National Army, late of Upper Merrion Street, Dublin and not Portobello Barracks, where he resided for the last six weeks of his life as head of the army. Upper Merrion Street was the address where the new Provisional Free State government had, earlier that year, taken up its headquarters. Michael was still a member of Dáil Eireann, and TD for both West Cork and Armagh and had only stepped down from being chairman of the Provisional Government when he became Commander-in-Chief of the National Army on 12 July.

In the last twenty years the number of people who come each year to pay their respects to one of Ireland's greatest leaders has increased, especially since 1996, when Neil Jordan introduced Michael Collins to the world with his film, portrayed by another Irishman, Liam Neeson. In the film, some mistakes were made. For example, the death of Harry Boland in the sewers of Dublin – he was shot in the stomach by a Free State soldier at the Grand Hotel, Skerries. Or the death of Ned Broy, who in fact was to become one of the first commissioners of the garda siochána under De Valera, and to survive into his mid eighties. However, despite the odd historical error, the film brought not only the character, and but also the sheer charisma and dynamism of Michael to millions on the silver screen.

Neil Jordan's film also aroused a new and further interest in Michael, not only in his native Ireland but also in Britain, America and around the world. Biographies about him were republished along with a renewed interest in many other books associated with him and his times such as Ernie O'Malley's *On Another Man's Wounds* and Tom Barry's *Guerrilla Days in Ireland.* Perhaps the most authoritative biography ever written about Michael was by Tim Pat Coogan. Originally published in 1990, the centenary of Michael's birth, it was republished in 1996 to coincide with the release of the film. It was also the book that initially sparked off my personal interest and fascination in Michael Collins. The film became the most successful ever made in Ireland, surpassing even John Wayne's classic *The Quiet Man.*

In January 2000, Michael voted as the 'number one' Irishman of the twentieth century, and has remained near the top ever since.

Whilst on the subject of Neil Jordan's film, one question I am often asked is why Liam Neeson, in his role as Michael, frequently used expletives and especially the 'F' word, when surely the real Michael would not have done so! I have to quickly disillusion people by telling them that Michael frequently swore and cursed, including the 'F' word, although rarely in front of women, unless they had done something to really annoy him. There are a couple of well-documented occasions when this happened. One was at the funeral of McKee and Clancy held a few days after Bloody Sunday on 25 November 1920, where Michael, wearing, unusually for him, a trenchcoat, was also one of the bearers. After the funeral mass at the Pro-Cathedral, he went on up to Glasnevin cemetery to attend the burials of his two former comrades. Suddenly a woman in the crowd recognised him, standing beside the graves and shouted: 'Oh look, there's Mick Collins!'

Michael, turning around, snarled back: 'Shut up you fucking bitch!'

Fortunately, there were no 'G' men or Auxiliaries around at the time and he was able to slip away quietly.

The other known occasion when Michael swore at a woman was after he had ordered one of his 'killings'. During and after the event he was always in a very emotional, pent-up state, sniping and baiting those around him, and on this particular occasion, took it out on Joe O'Reilly. After some hours of particularly cruel baiting Joe could stand it no more and told Michael he was going home. Michael, snarling at him said: 'All right, but take some of those dispatches with you on your way.' Joe dutifully delivered the papers to the woman they were addressed to, who immediately saw that Joe was very upset and had been crying. When she heard what had happened, she stormed straight over to Michael's office.

Michael shouted back at her: 'you mind your own fucking business. I know how O'Reilly works!'

The woman, totally taken aback, left immediately. Joe however returned to work the following day, and the whole incident was forgotten.

Whilst of the subject of films, Michael was also to be featured in two others, both made for television. First to be released and shown, was the excellent film *The Treaty*, produced by Thames Television/RTE in 1992, coinciding with its seventieth anniversary, and featuring Brendan Gleeson as a very lively and believable Michael. Then in January 2001, there was the RTE/BBC production of *Rebel Heart* about the experiences of a young Irishman from 1916 to 1922. Brendan Coyle excellently portrayed Collins.

The recent unveiling of the Michael Collins memorial statue in Clonakilty by Liam Neeson on 22 August 2002, eighty years to the day he was killed, was yet another occasion to show Michael was, and still is, one of Ireland's most popular heroes of the twentieth century (see page 126). The event drew a crowd of over 5,000, not only from the four corners of Ireland, but also Britain, Europe and America. Liam flew in to Cork airport that morning from New York. Many stirring speeches were given praising Michael and all he had done for Ireland and his significance today, including an excellent address from Tim Pat Coogan. Other speakers included the Leader of Fine Gael, Enda Kenny, TD, and the Fianna Fáil Agriculture

Minister, Joe Walsh, TD. Both politicians acknowledged Michael's inspirational influence and organising genius during the War of Independence, which had contributed to Ireland's eventual freedom from Britain. Again, it was an example of how Civil War politics had finally been laid to rest.

The bronze seven-foot statue of Michael, set upon a granite pedestal was erected in Emmet Square. He lived at No. 7 with his sister Margaret and her family for eighteen months, whilst attending the local national school in Clonakilty before going to London to work in July 1906. The statue portrays Michael, not as a soldier but as a civilian, as he still was on 15 June 1922, the day before the general election was called to vote for, or against, the Treaty. He appears as he did in an old cine film and press photographs taken of him the same day, as he addressed the crowds outside O'Donovan's Hotel in Pearse Street. The wording on the statue is simple and non-political. On the front is displayed just his name, date of birth and death, and his signature. At the rear is the following:

> *This monument is dedicated*
> *To the memory of*
> *Michael Collins*
> *And all those who*
> *Contributed to the*
> *Struggle for Irish*
> *National Self-Determination*
> *During the Easter Rising*
> *The War of Independence*
> *And the Civil War*
> *1916 to 1923.*

It also shows the last entry in his Field Diary – 21 August 1922:

> *The People are Splendid.*

I am aware of only two other statues of Michael in Ireland. There is the very attractive one in the grounds of the Civic Park in Cork city and the not so impressive example in Merrion Square, Dublin. Once, upon commenting to a colleague on the lack of statues of Michael around the country, I was reminded that there are very few, if any, of the men connected with the War of Independence. For example, despite his life-long involvement in Irish politics, spanning nearly sixty years, during which he served as taoiseach three times, and president twice, there is only one bronze statue erected to Eamon de Valera. This stands outside the courthouse in Ennis, Co. Clare – where he was a TD for over 40 years.

There have of course over the years been numerous television documentaries about the Easter Rising, the War of Independence and the Civil War and Michael is usually featured, if only briefly, in most of them. However, two that were made specifically about him come to mind. Kenneth Griffith's *Hang Up Your Brightest Colours* produced in the mid 1960s and banned in Britain as Griffith frequently refers to Britain's cruel and inhuman treatment of the Irish over the centuries. It is, however, an interesting portrayal of Michael and his life and times, although not always accurate. It also shows places connected with him, such as the huts at Frongoch in North Wales, that have now disappeared, as well as rare film footage, used for propaganda purposes at the time.

The second, produced by RTE in 1988, is Colm Connolly's excellent documentary *The Shadow of Beál na mBláth*. This two-hour film, in four parts, is a fascinating, in-depth study of Michael and the events that shaped his life. It too contains rare film footage and a re-inaction of Beál na mBláth ambush, as well as interviews with people who were alive at the time. It also touches on Michael's romance with Kitty and his possible affair with Hazel Lavery. The last part deals entirely with the events that surrounded Michael's death, using forensic evidence and information that had recently become known.

I suppose, to sum up Michael's relevance in modern day Ireland, I only need to reflect over the last six years that I have been researching and writing this book and the enthusiasm, interest and help I have received from people of all ages, just by mentioning that magic name, Michael Collins. One incident will always stand out in my memory.

I was trying to find the Wicklow Hotel in Wicklow Street, Dublin, a place often frequented by Michael around 1921 and early 1922. The jewellers Wier & Son, next door to the hotel, on the corner of Wicklow and Grafton Streets, is still there, where he bought Kitty's 'unofficial' engagement present, the watch. Sadly, however, the Wicklow Hotel is no more, although its sister hotel, The Central, down the road in Exchequer Street, has survived. Today, what was the Wicklow Hotel has now been taken over by Tower Records. Closing my ears to the pulsating sounds that hit you as you walk through the door, I went in to see if any trace of the old hotel was left. Ascending the stairs to the first floor, I noticed above my head the domed shaped cavity of an old Victorian skylight in the ceiling, of what was originally the landing of the hotel. This had somehow survived, and was something Michael Collins frequently passed under. I turned to the young, spiky haired, body pierced, assistants behind the counter and told them briefly about Michael's connection with the place. They were totally astounded and amazed that their shop was associated with THE Michael Collins!

Although newspapers were the main media, by 1921–22 film news bulletins were also being shown at local cinemas, and were being seen and enjoyed by the masses. Film newsreels along with newspapers carrying photographs covering topical political events in Ireland, such as Michael's involvement with the Treaty, his role as Chairman of the new Provisional Government and later as Commander-in-Chief, had through this new media, helped boost his image and introduced him to the general public. He was by August 1922, to the majority of the Irish population, well on the way to being a political 'rock star' and was in fact named 'Ireland's Idol' by the press just two days after he was shot. His early death was to leave him unsullied and still beautiful in many people's memories. He was the young, sexy, ebullient man who represented a liberated, unsanctimonious future for Ireland but due to one bullet, that future was never to be.

Today, he is once again Ireland's best-remembered charismatic leader. Whatever political party or creed one belongs to, it is generally acknowledged that he was the one man that helped to change the course of Irish history. He became a legend to champions of freedom for generations to come and admired the world over for his leadership skills.

Michael Collins was to become Ireland's greatest hero of the twentieth century.

FAMILY TREE

Father – Michael John Collins (Woodfield) b. 1815 d. 1897.
Mother – Mary Ann Collins *nee* O'Brien (Tullineasky) b. 1852 d. 1907.
Married 26 February 1876 at Rosscarbery and had 8 children.

Brothers – Johnny (Seán) Collins b. 1878 d. 1965.
    First wife Catherine (Katty) Hurley Drinagh b.? d. 1921.
    8 children: Donal, Mary, Kitty, Nellie, Seán, Liam, Joan (later Bunworth) and Pat.
    Second wife Nancy O'Brien (Carrigroe) b. 1882 d. 1962.
    2 children: Michael Collins (Waterford) and Nancy Collins-Hurley (Dublin).

    Patrick b. 1884 d. ? married Emma Jewel – 1 child who emigrated to America.

Sisters – Margaret b. 1877 d. 1954 married Patrick O'Driscoll – 13 children.
    Fachtna, Mary, Fionan, Ita, John, William, Patrick, Finola, Patricia, Michael, Breda, Una and Eva.

    Johanna (Hannie) b. 1879 d. 1971, worked for the post office in London where Michael joined her from 1906 to 1916.

    Mary b. 1881 d. 1955 married Patrick Powell – 9 children.
    Seán (later General Collins-Powell), Una, Mary-Clare, Maeve, Patrick, Brenda, Joan, Michael and Nora.

    Helena b. 1883 d. 1972 later Sister Mary Celestine of the Sisters of Mercy, Whitby, Yorkshire

    Katherine (Katie) b. 1887 d. 1964 married Joe Sheridan – no children.

MICHAEL'S EXTENDED FAMILY INCLUDED:

Bridget Butterley (*nee* O'Sullivan-Collins) was Michael's aunt in Howth. Bridget's mother was Margaret O'Sullivan (Castleventry) who married John Collins, Michael's grandfather. It is possible that Margaret was a widow and John Collins was her second husband and that Bridget and her two sisters Minnie and Nell were 'step' sisters to Michael's father. Bridget came to the Dublin area from West Cork and later married Jeremiah Butterley from Baldoyle. They had one daughter Mary, born 1894, Michael's first cousin. She later married a John Joseph Boland – no relation to Harry Boland. Joan Browne is her grand-daughter.

Bridget Butterley's two sisters Minnie and Nell also came to Dublin. Minnie became Mrs Dearham after marrying a wealthy farmer who ran an 800 acre farm in Stillorgan. They had no children and after her husband died, Minnie moved into a suite at the Shelbourne Hotel in Dublin and lived there for the rest of her life. Michael's other aunt Nell, also married a wealthy man called Keating and with their only daughter Kitty, lived in Baggot Roth House in Ballsbridge, Dublin. They owned Booth's China Warehouse in Middle Abbey Street, Dublin, next door to Harry Boland's tailoring shop at No. 64. These two aunts were very helpful to Michael during the War of Independence, letting him use their homes as safe-houses, as well as supporting him financially in various fund-raising schemes.

Michael Collins of Castlefreke, West Cork. His father Jim was born in 1888 and was first cousin to Michael on his father's side.

Nancy O'Brien of Carrigroe was born in 1882, and a second cousin to Michael, related to him on his mother's side. She later married his brother Johnny.

Seán Hurley, a second cousin of Michael's, related to Catherine Hurley, Johnny Collins' first wife. Knew Michael in London and died in 1916.

Kate O'Brien, Ownahincha, aunt of Michael's, married to one of his mother's brothers.

Mrs O'Brien Twohig, another aunt of Michael's, a sister of his mother. Lived in Haddon Road, Clontarf and Greystones, Co. Wicklow.

Peg O'Driscoll, *nee* O'Brien, and Jim O'Brien her brother are both second cousins to Michael, born and reared on the family farm at Sams Cross, where Jim still lives with his family. Their father Michael, born in 1890, was first cousin to Michael on his father's side. The two boys grew up together but as with the rest of Michael's relations and friends, were to see little of him after 1906 when he went to England to work and live. However, Michael always kept in touch with his family and was to spend his last Christmas at the O'Brien's farm at Sams Cross, along with his brother Johnny, who had been living there since the burning of Woodfield in April 1921.

Julia O'Donovan, *nee* Barry, originally from Skibbereen, later 16 Airfield Road, Dublin. An aunt of Gearóid O'Sullivan and a relation of Michael's on his uncle James' wife side of the family.

Fionnuala Donovan, grand-daughter of Julia and daughter of Sheila Donovan.

Gearóid O'Sullivan born Colnagrane, Skibbereen, distant cousin of Michael's on his father's mother's side.

Pol Ó Murchú, grand-nephew of Michael, grand-son of Margaret Collins-O'Driscoll.

Maureen Kirwin, grand-niece of Michael's, grand-daughter of Margaret Collins-O'Driscoll.

Patsy Fallon, grand-niece of Michael's, grand-daughter of Margaret Collins-O'Driscoll.

Mary-Clare O'Malley *nee* Collins-Powell, grand-niece of Michael's, daughter of Gen. Seán Collins-Powell, and grand-daughter of Mary Collins-Powell.

Nora Owen, grand-niece of Michael's, grand-daughter of Johnny Collins.

Mary Banotti (MEP) sister of Nora's and grand-daughter of Johnny Collins.

Joan Bunworth, *nee* Collins, niece to Michael and daughter of Johnny Collins and his first wife Catherine.

THE KIERNAN CONNECTIONS

Michael Collins Cronin, younger son of Kitty and Felix Cronin.

Laurette Kiernan, daughter of Larry Kiernan and Peggy *nee* Sheridan, niece of Kitty Kiernan.

Margot Gearty, *nee* Kiernan, sister of Laurette.

MICHAEL COLLINS: THE MAN WHO WON THE WAR
T. Ryle Dwyer

This is the story of a charismatic rebel who undermined British morale and inspired Irish people with exploits, both real and imaginary. Collins probably never killed anybody himself, but he did order the deaths of people standing in his way, and even advocated kidnapping an American president. He was the prototype on the urban terrorist and the real architect of the Black and Tan War.

MICHAEL COLLINS AND THE MAKING OF THE IRISH STATE
edited by Gabriel Doherty and Dermot Keogh

Collins has generally been portrayed in writing and film as a revolutionary guerrilla leader, a military tactician and a figure of great personal charm, courage and ingenuity. This collection of essays challenges that over-simplified view. It is a professional evaluation of Michael Collins and his contribution to the making of the Irish state, which brings to light his multifaceted and complex character. With contributions from many leading historians working in the field, and written in an accessible style, the essays make full use of archival material and provide new findings and insights into the life and times of Michael Collins.

THE SHOOTING OF MICHAEL COLLINS: MURDER OR ACCIDENT?
John M. Feehan

Was Michael Collins killed by an accident of war or was he ruthlessly murdered? Both of these possibilities are examined by the author, who has rejected the traditional theory that he was killed as a result of a ricochet bullet and leans towards the possibility that he was shot by a Mauser pistol.

THE GREAT IRISH FAMINE
Edited by Cathal Póirtéir

This is the most wide-ranging series of essays ever published on the Great Irish Famine and will prove of lasting interest to the general reader. Leading historians, economists, geographers – from Ireland, Britain and the United States – have assembled the most up-to-date research from a wide spectrum of disciplines, including medicine, folklore and literature, to give the fullest account yet of the background and consequences of the Famine.